STUDYING
HISTORY
How and Why

STUDYING HISTORY

How and Why

2nd edition

ROBERT V. DANIELS
University of Vermont

Prentice-Hall, Inc., Englewood Cliffs, New Jersey

TO ALICE,
For Our Partnership

ISBN: 0-13-858779-5

Library of Congress Catalog Card Number: 70-184844

Printed in the United States of America

10 9 8 7 6 5 4 3 2 1

PRENTICE-HALL INTERNATIONAL, INC., *London*
PRENTICE-HALL OF AUSTRALIA, PTY. LTD., *Sydney*
PRENTICE-HALL OF CANADA, LTD., *Toronto*
PRENTICE-HALL OF INDIA PRIVATE LIMITED, *New Delhi*
PRENTICE-HALL OF JAPAN, INC., *Tokyo*

CONTENTS

PREFACE

ALMOST EVERY FALL for a good many years I have had to face a captive audience of college students and try to justify the study of history. Naturally, I have attempted to explain the value of history as a basic part of the "liberal arts" education. But in doing this I realized that I needed to make more explicit the transfer values of mental training that history can yield. Further, I found it necessary to illustrate to my students in very basic terms the ways that history is organized, explained, and utilized by historians.

In the course of these efforts I became aware that most students at the college freshman level have little awareness of how history works, and cannot put historical facts into meaningful use. Worse, many students have been conditioned to regard history as a mass of facts with definite boundaries, all to be memorized, and all deadly dull. It was the recognition of these difficulties that led me to undertake the present book, to develop explicitly the awareness and approach that the instructor usually assumes his students to have—a background that the instructor must assume, if he is to have time to teach his course. The book is aimed primarily at college freshmen and sophomores to answer just this need for foundation, although I hope it will prove meaningful to younger students and perhaps also to more mature readers who want to know how to make sense of history. Prospective teachers may find this book of some value in preparing to make history meaningful in high school. However, I have not attempted to reach the level of a text for the specialized historiography course for history majors.

I have begun this introduction to history with a resume of the values and uses that may be derived from studying history. This is followed with an explanation—new to many students—of the ways in which history is classified and taught, and the place it holds in the world of learning in relation to the social sciences and humanities. I then turn to the practical problems of how the student goes about taking a course, assimilating a segment of history, and organizing information to develop his understanding. Following this are two chapters on the active side of historical study—writing and research. I have found it particularly important to give students this sort of experience, and to prepare them for it by clear explanation of the fundamental scholarly procedures. This I believe to be the most direct way to convey an understanding of the spirit of history and a respect for its accomplishments.

Lastly I have touched on some of the philosophical problems of comprehending the past—historical relativity, causation, the role of individuals, and the multifactor nature of historical reality.

Acknowledgments

In a sense this book is not the work of an individual at all, because I have drawn so much on the published thoughts and unpublished consensus of other members of the historical profession. To a few people I am particularly indebted, for their critical reading, suggestions, and encouragement—David Newhall, Lester Jipp, Evan G. Coe, Stanley Evans, and my wife, Alice Daniels. I am grateful to Marjorie Dalton, Hazel Elliott, and Carolyn Perry for their labors in typing the manuscript, to R. G. Fleig for a fine job of editing, and to Warren A. Beck and Achilles Avramides for their very helpful critique in detail. I hope that, thanks to the help I have had, my work does not seem too much a tour de force either of principle or of presentation.

This second edition of *Studying History* has been extensively revised, particularly the last chapter and wherever the presentation appeared to need more clarity. I am indebted to the numerous users of the first edition who kindly made available their comments and criticisms.

R.V.D.

**TO
THE
STUDENT**

THE PURPOSE OF THIS BOOK is to explain how you go about studying history—and why. It is an attempt to put down in black and white all the methods and objectives that historians take for granted and don't usually bother to explain, even though these points have not often occurred to most beginning students or readers. I hope that this book will enable you as a student or reader of history to attune your mind to appreciate better what your teacher or author is trying to do.

Unfortunately the study of history usually involves certain problems that make the subject seem difficult or boring. It is neither. To make history accessible and interesting by explaining these problems is the object of this book. One such problem is the use of factual details, which should be used in the pursuit of significance rather than learned as ends in themselves. There is the problem of organization, which encompasses the entire subject—the organization of facts in relation to ideas, the classification of past events into different types and areas, the planning of the work involved in research and writing. There are philosophical problems of understanding history. Is it a science? If not, what is it? How can you go about explaining anything? Finally, what good is the study of history? How does it actually accomplish the direct and indirect benefits that I have suggested here? These questions are the hurdles that must be passed on the road to a true appreciation of history, and my purpose in the chapters that follow is to help you surmount these hurdles successfully.

I suggest that you read this book slowly and study it carefully wherever you find unfamiliar points. It contains many ideas and a good deal of advice that will take time and practical application to absorb fully. For this reason, it is best to work through the book a chapter at a time, along with your course of study or your reading, and look for examples in your work to illustrate the points being made in the book. Once you get the spirit of the approach presented here and develop some new habits of thought and study, history should become a new and vital experience for you.

1

THE USES
OF
HISTORY

—HISTORY IS THE MEMORY of human group experience. If it is forgotten or ignored, we cease in that measure to be human. Without history we have no knowledge of who we are or how we came to be, like victims of collective amnesia groping in the dark for our identity. It is the events recorded in history that have generated all the emotions, the values, the ideals that make life meaningful, that have given men something to live for, struggle over, die for. Historical events have created all the basic human groupings—countries, religions, classes —and all the loyalties that attach to these. History is a source of inspiration as it holds up to us the tradition and the glory, the clashing passions and heroic exploits of past generations. In it we find the drama of real life. In written form it is a branch of literature, an entertaining art whose special appeal is that its material is true.

History deserves to be studied out of curiosity if nothing else. The record of man's past offers a challenge for inquiry and understanding no less stimulating than the mysteries of outer space and subatomic matter which absorb the attention of the pure scientist, whether his investigation promises to yield practical results or not. It is a field of intellectual exploration and adventure, and therefore a source of satisfaction for these fundamental human yearnings.

Does History Teach Lessons?

Like the pure pursuit of science, the pure study of history can have immense practical significance.—A person must know some history if he is even to begin to understand the world he lives in, or to act with any wisdom and perspective. History is the record of all experience. The present is only a fleeting instant, and everything we are conscious of is already in the past, has already become a part of history.—Intelligent action is based on learning from past experience, and thus it is in history of one sort or another that we must seek whatever

answers we may hope to find about the conduct of human affairs, personally no less than publicly.

"The-lessons-of-history" is a familiar phrase, so much so that the lessons are sometimes learned too well. History never repeats itself exactly. No historical situation is the same as any other; even two like events differ in that the first has no precedent, while the second has. But even in this respect history can teach a lesson—nothing ever stays the same. "You cannot step twice into the same river," said the ancient Greek philosopher Heraclitus, "for fresh waters are ever flowing in upon you." The only unchanging thing in human affairs is the constancy of change itself.

The process of history is unique, but nonetheless intelligible. Each situation and event is distinct, but each is connected to all the foregoing and succeeding ones by a complex web of cause and effect, probability and accident. The present may be the consequence of accidents, or of irresistible forces, but in either case the present consequences of past events are real and irreversible. The unique present, just as each unique point in the past, is utterly unintelligible unless we understand the history of how it came to be.

While history is a record of unique happenings, it is something more than chaos. To perceive the elements of order in the chaotic record of past events is the distinctive task of the historian. Events, people, groups, institutions fall into certain classes that exhibit at least partial regularities. We can use the words *France, king, war, frontier* independently of particular times and people and still know more or less what we are talking about. On a broader scale the historian can conceive of historical "trends" or "processes," where one event leads to another in a more or less logical way. Thinking in such terms is very important when it comes to understanding how the present—which is really the immediate, perceivable past —has grown out of the more remote past. The same approach is the only way in which we can rationally anticipate the future—to observe the processes of change or development that appear to have been going on up to now and to project them into the future, i.e., to guess what will happen if they continue in the same way.

Professional historians do not have any monopoly on the thoughtful study of human affairs. All of the other social sciences and humanities are engaged in this, though people in each discipline work from their own particular standpoint. History, however, must be drawn upon by all other fields. It offers the raw record of what has happened, and it sets the context of unique situations in the stream of time within which the other forms of specialized inquiry must operate.

This outward-looking emphasis on the broad range of human affairs does not exhaust the value of history. The study of history is important not only for what it tells us about our world, but also for its value in developing our powers of thinking. Successful historical study forces us to train and exercise all the essential aspects of intellectual activity—it excites curiosity and the spirit of inquiry; it disciplines the faculty of reason; it cultivates the arts of self-expression and communication. Historical study is also fundamental in developing the attitudes of mind that distinguish the educated man—the habits of skepticism and criticism; of thinking with perspective and objectivity; of judging the good and the bad and the in-between in human affairs; of weighing the pros and cons and discerning the different shades of gray that lie between the white and the black. Historical study is fundamental in attaining wisdom and the values of the educated man.

History and Liberal Education

The objective of most school and college study—the goal summed up in the terms "general education" or "liberal education"—is often misunderstood. It is not direct preparation for a particular skill or employment, but a more indirect aim, an investment, as it were, in knowledge, frames of reference, and the ability to think and express oneself. Such an educational background can be important throughout life, and even more so as a person rises to positions involving responsibility and judgment.

A liberal education particularly involves the development of perspective, so that a person can see himself in relation to the rest of the human experience as well as the natural universe. History, above all, means perspective—the view of human events in their total setting of time, place, and institutions. An educated conception of oneself and mankind is impossible without the perspective afforded by a basic knowledge of the past.

The values of a liberal education, especially the mental training which is its basis, are difficult to impart directly and in the abstract. This is why they are usually approached through specific subjects that the student learns to think about. The subject chosen is not as important as the effort to think systematically about the subject, to use it as a gnawing bone to help cut the mental teeth of neophyte thinkers. This is a value found in all of the various liberal arts.

History is particularly rich in the opportunity it offers for learning how to think, thanks to the challenges inherent in its subject matter and to the strong tradition among historians of cultivating the general powers of the intellect. The techniques of historical thinking have a high carry-over value for other subjects and activities. They are general mental skills that everyone should acquire in order to be effectively educated.

—Historical study requires constant exercise in the relationship of details and generalizations.—It gives experience in the organization and classification of extensive data.—It teaches the student how to look for relevant information and to use it in solving problems. If you approach it right, history teaches you how not to be swamped by details that will soon be forgotten, but rather how to use them in order to develop understanding.

—History teaches judgment.—It does this both by supplying a knowledgeable background and by training in the technique of criticism and reasoned conclusions. Good judgment often depends upon asking the right questions, and the knack for this depends upon the use of a disciplined imagination. Sometimes, in the absence of clear or consistent information, judgment must be reserved, as many an historical problem illustrates.—A healthy skepticism, though never cynicism, should be one aim of all historical instruction.

As a subject of unlimited inquiry, history can be a powerful stimulant to the curiosity and the thirst for truth. The spirit of historical inquiry is enlivened by its legitimate subjective side in the play of individual opinion, values, and imagination. The student learns that his own opinion is worthwhile, provided only that he has based it on knowledge and is ready to revise it when new knowledge makes this necessary. More like the humanities than the sciences, work in history is always a personal intellectual venture.

Historical study is good training in dealing with complexity. All the simple historical facts and concepts are really very complex abstractions referring to hosts of actions and events. On the other hand, history demonstrates how necessary it is to reduce a complex topic to a relatively few manageable concepts, such as process or trend, in order to think at all meaningfully.—History shows how facts and ideas must be used together, the ideas developed from a knowledge of the facts and checked against them, while the facts are organized and interpreted in relation to the ideas that give them meaning.

History, if taught right, is never cut and dried. There is always more information that can be unearthed, and imaginative new interpretations may be possible on any topic, new or old. But successful inquiry needs more than curiosity and enthusiasm. It demands a rigorous method, to assure the effective collection, selection, and organization of information, and to replace gullibility with skepticism. These are habits of mind that are indispensable in any responsible occupation in today's complex world.

The Historical Approach

The most distinctive feature of the historical approach is its emphasis on the time dimension. The sense of time is a reminder that the present is the product of the past, and also a transitory point in an ongoing evolutionary process. History teaches just how transitory much that today appears to be permanent will probably turn out to be, as well as the reality of much that survives from the past.[1]

Emphasis on the time dimension forces us to weigh the significance of events and ideas in relation to their particular historical setting. What is a significant novelty for one epoch —bookkeeping or fur trading, for instance—is in a later epoch an established routine unnoticed by history. Ideas that are radical spearheads in one century—nationalism and laissez faire a hundred and fifty years ago, for example—become the redoubts of a reactionary rearguard in later times. Ideas that seem perfectly natural in the present—democracy and social security—were impossible, utopian dreams a few centuries or even a few decades ago. The orthodoxies of the present will likely fade and wither, while the dreams and struggles of the moment will become the familiar possessions of blasé generations to come. Because the significance of an idea or institution depends on its setting in time, an historical perspective is basic in the study of all social sciences and humanities.

Along with the perspective of the time dimension, historical study involves a breadth of view over all the aspects of human behavior. While specialized study in the social sciences properly requires the abstraction of one distinct aspect of life— political, economic, social, etc.—from the living whole, at some point a corrective is needed to put the specialized insights back into an integrated picture of mankind. This history attempts to do. It allows no single-factor interpretations, but requires that motives and circumstances in all aspects of life be given their due weight in explaining human experience.

History engenders an awareness that events do not often follow human plans, and that the results of action seldom correspond fully with its intent. The student of history is therefore likely to recognize the discrepancies between ideologies

---

[1] To feel the reality of the past it helps very much to visit the places where historic events actually occurred. There is more opportunity for this in Europe than in America, but in most parts of the United States there are historic buildings, restored forts, and occasional battlefields. Even old cemeteries document the age of a town and serve to remind us that the past is just as real as the present.

and systems, between theory and practice. He can appreciate
how people in all countries and all walks of life can ration-
alize their motives with ideas that don't really correspond to
reality. History points up some of the limitations of man's
rationality.

The ultimate virtue of the historical approach is the detachment that enables the observer to rise above human conflicts and see all sides of a question, no matter which position
he personally prefers. Historical study teaches the recognition of legitimate differences of viewpoint and the difficulty
of final judgments in human affairs. Historical thinking ap-
preciates the mixture of motives and the balance of wisdom
and error in any human situation. Who was right in the
American Civil War, the North or the South? The question as
put is meaningless, because the practical significance of
"right" depends on its setting in time, and because either-or
judgments are an affront to historical reality. Good historical
study recognizes how rarely, if ever, clear-cut conflicts occur
between good and evil, black and white. It also recognizes
the differences among the many distinct shades of gray. This
is the most important lesson that history can offer its students
for coping with their own world.

History and Citizenship

In this age of mass education through the secondary and even
the college levels, one of the major tasks (and opportunities)
of teaching is to prepare the student to be an informed and
conscientious citizen, to play his part as a responsible member
of a democratic society, and very likely to assume the role
of intelligent leadership. History, perhaps more than any
other single discipline, is the natural vehicle for instruction
in these responsibilities. The subject matter of history affords
the essential perspective for the citizen to understand what is
going on in his world, and the method of historical thinking
is the best kind of training in the virtues of reasoned judgment.

Since the dawn of civilization, in almost every society,

history has been regarded as the natural vehicle for teaching the private citizen the public virtues of loyalty and responsibility. To a degree this function contradicts the emphasis we have just placed on history as training in critical judgment and detachment. It is always tempting to the leaders of governments or movements to use history as propaganda. Much traditional teaching of history everywhere in the world, especially below the university level, has had the purpose of indoctrination—particularly of glorifying the national state and conditioning school children to an automatic loyalty to the nation. With this end in view, the study of national history has often been required by law.

More often than not, the writing of national history has been chauvinistic and one-sided, justifying that nation's achievements and ambitions and glossing over or explaining away its shortcomings and failures. It cultivates a mythology about the nation's origins and leaders as all-wise and even sacrosanct (e.g., the American Founding Fathers), if not actually divine (the creation of Japan by the god Izanagi and the goddess Izanami). Perhaps the urge to make one's own heroes look pure and good and to blacken the enemy is a natural human trait. But this helps explain how the vested interests of traditional national history can become a substantial obstacle to the dissemination of the real values of historical study in its reflective and objective quest for truth.

National history is not the only source of resistance to objective inquiry. Much worse, in recent decades, have been the ideological movements of Communism and Fascism, with their commitments to certain absolute visions of the past, present, and future. Not only do these movements censor historical thoughts that contradict their own preconceived doctrines, but they produce official, rewritten versions of history in which all manner of distortion, half-truths, lies, and suppression of fact are employed to justify the movement, its power, its leaders, and even its particular policies of the moment. History under these circumstances becomes purely an instrument of political propaganda.

Similar pitfalls exist where history is being reinvestigated to lend identity to an ethnic group—Black history in the United States, for instance—or to justify a political stand, as in the New Left and ultra-Right critiques of American foreign policy. This is not to suggest that such topics should be avoided—it is vital to correct the sins of omission left over by past historians—but rather to point out the need to avoid self-serving distortions, and to pursue the facts of history as objectively as possible.

On the positive side, is there any way that honest historical inquiry can serve the body politic? The answer is emphatically yes, on condition that society and its leaders are sufficiently openminded to appreciate the complexities of history and to accept unpleasant facts and interpretations. The nation that can dispense with self-glorification and look at itself and the world with a true historical approach has taken a long step toward wisdom. Perhaps Great Britain illustrates this quality today more than any other major country.

National history has a vital part to play in promoting a country's mature self-awareness, provided only that it is taught and studied in a spirit of objectivity, which is in turn facilitated by historical perspective. National history, therefore, should be studied not in isolation, but in the context of parallel or divergent developments in other countries and of the pertinent historical antecedents. United States history is sometimes approached as a unique phenomenon, giving the impression that neither capitalism nor democracy, for instance, have developed anywhere else. Ethnic history in America would be similarly enhanced in meaning by a comparative view of national and ethnic strivings around the world and in times past. A nation's citizens as well as its leaders need a clearer idea of what experiences and values they share with other lands, and in what respects, for better or worse, their country is different.

Granting a mature and objective attitude, historical understanding is obviously invaluable as a guide to statesmen in their efforts to manage the future. Historical study should be essential training for society's future leaders, whatever specialty they may pursue in the meantime. Many times, in fact, the profession of history has been the launching pad for famous political careers—to take a few, François Guizot, prime minister of France during the "July Monarchy"; the great leader of Russian liberalism, Paul Miliukov; Lester Pearson, prime minister of Canada; and several United States senators, including Democratic majority leader Mike Mansfield.

Historical awareness is important not only for the leaders, but for the citizenry as a whole if they are to choose intelligently, as they must in a democracy. The point is not to condition them to loyalty, as a dictatorship must; history should show, in fact, that the foundations of real loyalty and commitment rest not on indoctrination, but go deep down in the whole network of social life. What history can give the citizen of a democracy is a realistic perspective on the nature of his society, its problems, and the direction it is headed in. It can teach him patience for the short run, by showing that quick and complete solutions to national problems are unlikely, and it can make him ready to accept change in the long run, by showing that no way of life and no balance of political forces can ever stand still for long. Above all, history can inoculate the citizen against gullibility, against unthinking belief in the leader who promises either quick change or no change at all. We must look to history for the record of social experience that can help make the citizen the wise and responsible voter that democracy depends on.

2
FIELDS
OF
HISTORY

THE RECORD OF THE HUMAN PAST is vast and complicated. To begin to understand history it is easiest to take it one part at a time or find the segment of it that is most relevant to one's interests. To do this without disturbing the natural unity of the past it is important to recognize those segments of it within which people's lives have been particularly linked. Some of these segments are given us quite obviously, as with the political divisions—countries—within which most of mankind lives. Others are sliced off by historians in some way that makes sense to them—periods of time or different aspects of events. The student should understand these classes of historical information at the very beginning, and learn to use them for his own purposes.

Societies and Countries

When you look down at the world from an airplane at twenty or thirty thousand feet you begin to realize the vastness of human society and the miracle of the unseen network of human relationships that holds together countless thousands of farmsteads and hamlets, with occasional smoky heaps of cities, in what is ordinarily a stable, working system of society. Physical links are provided by transportation and communication systems—themselves radically changed over the course of history—but more profound are the economic links of exchange and the political ties provided by government. Government above all gives to a territory the social unity and the common experience that permit us to study its history as a country.

In modern times in the West, where the national state has prevailed, the national basis of history has been taken for granted. Each nation has furthermore tended to look at world history from its own particular standpoint. This emphasis on the past of one's own country has often led to a parochial lack of perspective or even a heavy propagandistic bias. This is how the French and Germans used to be taught about each other, and the Russians are so indoctrinated even today. Sometimes events give a peculiar character to the history of a part of one country. The American Civil War, for example, still cannot be viewed in the same light in the Northern and Southern states, and its historical effects are still felt in social and political differences that everyone must constantly take into account.

While national history has its pitfalls of bias and parochialism, it is a necessary approach to a civilization such as that of the modern West, where the historical experience has been primarily on national lines. It is perfectly natural that in the United States, American history should be taught in a separate course concentrating on the specific experience of the American past. Likewise the detailed study of European history for the advanced college student is offered in individual courses on the principal countries. In other cases the national approach breaks down for one reason or another. Latin American history is more effectively taught on a regional basis, since Spanish culture and the common Spanish colonial experience still link most of the region more than the various individual governments divide it. The history of India and Pakistan cannot be separated prior to independence in 1947; a country may be partitioned, but its previous common historical experience cannot be. Yugoslavia has the opposite problem in attempting to teach its school children a national history. Since there was no Yugoslavia before 1918, the past of every region now in the republic has to be traced, with historical threads everywhere from Austria and Venice to the Ottoman Empire.

For certain times and places social units are more basic than political ones. We can find nations, societies, cultures reflecting shared experiences that may continue despite every vicissitude of conquest or partition in the political realm. Poland did not cease to exist between the eighteenth and twentieth centuries, even though there was no Polish state in existence. India has been an historical entity for millennia, even though politically it has never been completely united and independent at the same time. The natural unit of study, be it a political or only a cultural entity, is itself determined by the particular history of a given place and period.

Sometimes we must deal with a more fundamental order of historical phenomena. This is what, for lack of a better term, is spoken of as "a civilization," that is, a particular way of life with certain characteristic institutions, values, beliefs, and the early background of one distinct and unifying religion, shared by people living in a wide area and over a long period of time. Civilizations have been regarded by the more speculative and philosophical historical thinkers as the primary unit of historical study. Numerous intriguing theories have been devised to explain the cyclical rise and fall of civilizations. The most famous are those of the German, Oswald Spengler (*The Decline of the West*) and the Englishman, Arnold Toynbee (*A Study of History*).

The theorists have differed in their estimate of what actually constitutes a distinct civilization, but for modern times it is easy to specify them: Western or European or West European civilization (including the Americas); the Moslem civilization of North Africa and the Middle East; Indian or Hindu civilization; and the Far Eastern civilization, embracing China and Japan. Where Russia fits in is not clear, least of all to the Russians themselves. Their background goes back to the fairly distinct Byzantine or Eastern Orthodox Christian civilization, but so much Europeanization has taken place in the past couple of centuries that Russia ought to be regarded in most respects as merely a peculiar part of the Western world. Each of these various civilizations is worth lifetimes of study. Each represents ways of living and thinking that are very difficult for an outsider to appreciate.

The history of a foreign civilization should be approached first by taking the entire civilization as a unit, complex though it may be. Such work on the Middle East, India, and the Far East is being increasingly offered in American universities. A corresponding overall approach to our own civilization is perhaps the most difficult challenge faced by teacher and student alike. Here we must strain to see the outline through the thicket of familiar detail; we must rise above the mental boundaries of party, faith, or nation, and try to appraise the experiences common to the West.

The typical survey course in Western civilization is only a beginning, though it can establish some of the fundamentals of the subject. The course should get Western civilization located for us in space and in time—from the fall of Rome to the present, from the rivers Bug and Una to the Atlantic Ocean (plus overseas colonization). The course should also establish the elements of common historical experience that make Western civilization a meaningful entity: the Graeco-Roman and Judaeo-Christian heritage; the religious unity of Roman Catholic Christendom prior to the Reformation; the permanent political disunity and perpetual counterbalancing of church and state, with the diversity, freedom, and change that all this allowed; the tension between authority and the individual; the irrepressible spirit of inquiry, exploration, and adventure that has brought the West to the pinnacle of power.

Historical Periods

The history of a long-lived national state, not to mention a major civilization, may sweep across many hundreds of years and involve vast changes in the life of the people concerned. Study that is to any degree detailed must therefore be divided into periods of time. These divisions do not have to be arbitrary ones, such as centuries. Actual turning points can be found, where the system of life or the political organization has rapidly changed. The fall of Rome is a turning point of such striking import that all thinking about European history must proceed from it. The independence of the United States is similarly a prime watershed in the history of North America.

Other divisions may become habitual, even though in a subsequent perspective they lose much of their significance. Such is the conventional distinction between the so-called Middle Ages and the modern world around 1500. While the changes associated with the Renaissance, the voyages of discovery, and the Reformation are not to be ignored, more fundamental changes occurred *within* the Middle Ages (the revival of commerce and culture in the eleventh and twelfth centuries) and within more modern times (the industrial revolution). The medieval-modern distinction obscures the underlying continuity in most aspects of Western life, especially the political and economic, between the fourteenth and eighteenth centuries.

So long as its limitations are understood, the division of history into periods must be employed as a framework for detailed inquiry. In the more remote history of a given civilization, periods are often more meaningful units of study than nations, for they represent phases of the common experience that all of the particular nations have gone through. Thus it is natural for the advanced university study of Western civilization to be divided on a period basis, with specialized courses on the "Middle Ages" (ending variously between 1300 and 1500); "Renaissance and Reformation," linking the late medieval and early modern eras; "modern Europe," with semesters of study from the Treaty of Westphalia in 1648 to the French Revolution or the fall of Napoleon, and from 1789 or 1815 to the outbreak of World War I; and "contemporary history," from World War I to the present. The last inevitably spills out over the limits of strictly European affairs into the world at large, which recent events have linked inescapably into a single historical entity.

Further subdivisions of time are usually made within

the frame of a particular country or problem. The history of the United States is typically divided into the colonial period; the revolutionary period from 1763 to 1789; the early national period, to 1815 or so; the "middle period" embracing the Jacksonian Revolution and the sectional struggle culminating in the Civil War; Reconstruction, extending to 1876; the "Gilded Age," to around 1900, and the Progressive Era, to World War I; the "Normalcy" of the 'twenties, up to the Great Depression; and the New Deal, to 1941. For more recent times, the outlines of history are less defined by professional consensus, and the best periodization that can be agreed on for any country's last few years is necessarily based on presidential administrations, prime ministerships, dictators' tenure from coup to coup, etc.

Aspects of Historical Experience

Sometimes, particularly in the study of brief periods in individual countries, the most meaningful division of the historical picture is topical, i.e., the separate study of the different forms of human relationships and activities that occur there. Within a particular area, over a limited span of time, a certain aspect of the life of society can have a distinct history, to a considerable degree independent of other things happening in the same society.

The topics or aspects among which historians divide their work are familiar and obvious: political, with subdivisions for diplomatic and military history; economic; social (often considered together with the economic); cultural and intellectual. Political history concentrates on governments and rulers and on what they accomplish by use of their authority both in relation to the people under their control and in their dealings with other governments and rulers. Economic history encompasses all the activities involved in producing goods and services—agriculture and industry, trade and transportation, technology and business organization. Social history is more amorphous, but includes the history of social institutions and relationships (ranging from the family to classes and nations), of typical conditions and customs, and of popular beliefs and movements. Cultural and intellectual history tends to concentrate on the individual work of the leading scholars and artists, but also extends to the realms of religion, education, science, literature, and philosophy. Recent historical work has shifted emphasis from the almost exclusively political and diplomatic interest that prevailed until the late nineteenth century, to place equal stress on the socioeconomic and cultural-intellectual areas of life.

Following in this direction, new fields of historical study may be shaped in response to the issues and problems that a society is experiencing in the present. The surge of interest in urban history and ethnic history (particularly Black history) in the United States is a case in point. Such specialties, cutting across the usual historical categories, underscore the flexibility of historians' conceptions and the readiness with which the historical approach can be made relevant to the problems of the day.

All division of history into special interest areas, however, is a matter of convenience, and should never be taken as an absolute. While it is important to distinguish between the various kinds or levels of historical activity and apportion emphasis properly among them, it is also necessary to keep in mind the interrelationships among them, not to mention the borderline events that may appear to be either political or economic, either social or cultural, depending upon the interests of the observer. All the different aspects of history are facets of human behavior and of the web of social life.

The character of each aspect of life is bound to be affected by what is happening on the other levels. Politics are affected by economics, and vice versa, by intellectual life, and vice versa. The interrelationships are exceedingly complicated and must be sorted out carefully and without prejudice in each instance. Economic life was long neglected, and this prompted Karl Marx, among others, to lay almost exclusive stress upon it in his "materialist" conception of history. However, this overemphasis on the influence of the economic side is equally unrealistic. Every form of human activity must be taken into account and must be seen in the larger context.

The Specialized Study of History

The introductory or survey course in history, even at the college level, can scarcely do more than scratch the surface of the historical record in its infinitely rich detail. Even the familiar advanced courses, concentrating on countries or periods, must of necessity leave many historical stones unturned. Half a loaf is nevertheless better than none, and whatever college work in history a student can manage to undertake, his perspective on human affairs will be that much clearer.

A student desiring to concentrate or major in history normally takes four or more one-year courses in the field, together with two or more courses in a related field of social science or the literature of the country he is interested in. The requirement for a major in American colleges and universities typically includes a survey of European history, either from the fall of Rome or from the Renaissance to the present time; a year's survey of United States history; and specialized courses chosen from the wide variety offered by most departments of history.

The period histories of the West that are usually offered are medieval, Renaissance and Reformation, modern European, and contemporary history. National histories most often include Great Britain, Russia, France, and Germany. Regional courses are given on Latin America and sometimes Eastern Europe. Histories of other civilizations are less common, except for ancient Greek and Roman history and occasionally that of the Far East. However, we have noted the strong tendency in American universities today to develop instruction in the history of the hitherto neglected areas of the world, especially South Asia, the Moslem world, and Africa.

Topical courses in history—diplomatic, economic, intellectual, scientific, religious—are also frequently offered. In the United States it is most common to divide the advanced study of American history in this fashion. State, regional, and ethnic histories, appropriate to the particular locality, also figure in the usual American history offering.

Specialization in history on the undergraduate level has direct professional application in the field of secondary education. For a high school teacher of history or social studies it is essential to have at least the equivalent of a college history major. For many other areas of work such a background provides valuable preparation, especially in law, journalism and communications, and government service. For graduate study leading to college teaching or research in the social sciences and humanities, a history background is often as advantageous as specific study in the field concerned.

To prepare for professional work in history at the advanced level—college teaching and research—systematic graduate training is naturally required. A master's degree may be earned after the first year or two of graduate study, but a permanent college teaching career is normally based on attainment of the doctor's degree or Ph.D. This involves at least two years of study in a variety of specialized history courses, seminars in which research practice begins, and a comprehensive examination, written or oral or both. Then follows the work of independent research and writing to prepare the thesis or dissertation. This requires at least a year of full-time effort, and often two or three years, to produce a book-length work of historical scholarship that must be an original contribution to knowledge and understanding in a particular area of inquiry. The doctor's degree demonstrates that its holder is an independent scholar, qualified to instruct advanced students and train new scholars in their turn. He is now a full-fledged historian, ready to take his part in the perpetuation and deepening of man's understanding of his past.

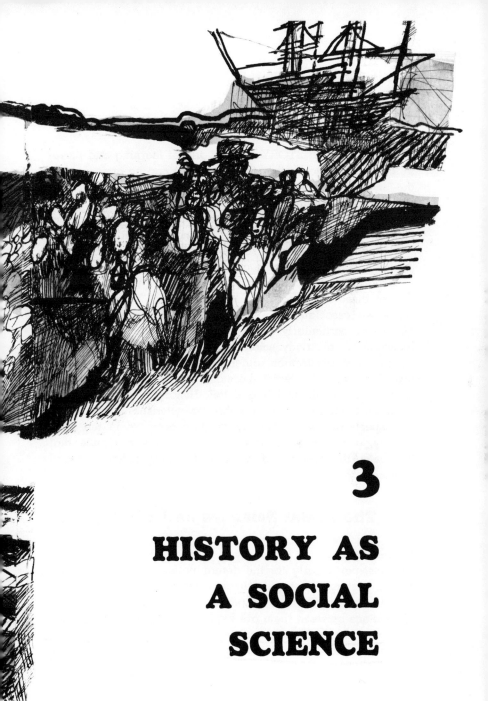

3

HISTORY AS
A SOCIAL
SCIENCE

THE PLACE OF HISTORY in the world of learning and its relation to the various other fields of study can be argued without end. History is sometimes classed with the humanities, along with literature, the arts, and philosophy, but it differs from all of these subjects in being based primarily on fact rather than on imagination and feeling. It is more often included among the social sciences, together with economics, political science, sociology, anthropology, and some branches of geography and psychology. One may question whether any of these fields deserves to be called a "science" in the sense we associate with the natural or exact sciences, but history is particularly distinguished from the others in its resistance to a strictly scientific approach. It tries to explain by particular description rather than by general analysis and laws; its aim is to depict the significant historical individual or situation in all its living detail. History is defined by its focus on time, but it also has the characteristic of embracing all aspects of human activity as they occurred in the past. History, accordingly, is able to serve as the discipline that integrates the specialized work of the other fields of social science.

The Social Sciences and History

In the usual three- or four-way classifications of academic subjects, particularly for the determination of course requirements, history is almost always thrown together with the social sciences. There is ample logic for this, so long as the distinctions between them are kept clear. History is a study of the facts of man's social existence, which is essentially the common denominator of the social sciences. History bears close relations to all the particular social sciences, and is really no more different from them in concept, method, and material than they are among each other.

Geography and political science are the fields most intimately related to history, to the extent of inevitable interpenetration and overlapping. Geography studies the terrestrial setting in which history has occurred, sets the spatial dimension of historical events, and endeavors to explain the relation between land forms and resources on the one hand and man's historical accomplishments on the other. Political science endeavors to explain analytically and systematically the same vast range of political data and events that constitute a major portion of our historical experience.

Economics and the behavioral sciences—sociology, anthropology, and psychology—deal with more specialized approaches or realms of experience: economics with the relations of production and exchange expressed by money; sociology with the web of informal as well as formal relationships among people; anthropology with the patterns of behavior and belief that distinguish particular societies; and psychology with thought, emotion, and behavior from the standpoint of the individual human being. The conclusions of all of these disciplines may constitute valuable insights for the historian, and must not be overlooked. Conversely, each of these disciplines must draw on the data of history and incorporate the perspective of history on the changing circumstances of human behavior. A notable recent influence of the social sciences on history is the expanding interest in quantitative approaches to historical research, particularly since the computer has greatly facilitated the utilization of statistical, political, and population data.

History plays an important part wherever interdisciplinary social science work has been developed. Foreign area studies, either on the undergraduate or graduate level, focus on a particular country or area of civilization, and combine the history of the area with its language and literature and with the analyses supplied by the other social sciences.

History as the Study of Particulars

The basic difference between history and the other social sciences is that the latter take individuals and events en masse, study the qualities they have in common, and arrive at general laws about human affairs, whereas history is the study of a unique sequence of individuals, events, situations, ideas, and institutions, occurring in the one-dimensional and irreversible stream of time. Since history is the study of particulars, it is impossible for the historian to proceed in the same way as the scentist, who tries to generalize from his observations and experiments to arrive at laws of natural phenomena. There are no laws of history in the strict sense, although there are of course many regularities and patterns in human behavior that, once established by the social scientists, must be taken into account by the historian in his investigations. All the historian can really do is to explain by careful description how an event occurred or how its consequences followed; he can never repeat an experiment in order to test what effect the presence or absence of a certain factor might have.

Not all particular events fall within the scope of history, which treats only of those events, institutions, personalities, and so forth that have historical significance—that is, that have enough effect on other events, institutions, and so forth to make them worth being remembered. A particular fact need not be unusual or spectacular to be of historical significance, but it must have power to exert a significant effect. Political organization is the most common system for magnifying small events into large consequences, such that the actions of leaders may dictate the future of a whole country. This, naturally, is why history must be first and foremost political history, and why it can get so closely concerned with the details of statecraft and rulers' private lives. A political decision or a diplomatic deal could decide the fate of whole nations, as they did, for example, at Vienna in 1815 and at Yalta and Potsdam in 1945. The outcome of a battle can depend on the weather or the health of a commander, and the future of a country often hangs in the balance. What, indeed, if General Grant had been thrown from his horse and killed during the siege of Vicksburg, as MacKinlay Kantor has speculated in his historical fantasy, If the South Had Won the Civil War? "For want of a nail, the kingdom was lost." This is no idle paradox, but true insight into the accidents that sometimes govern history.

With individuals as with events, it is their personal influence on the world around them that makes them historical figures. Such people are usually either political or intellectual leaders, who, by command of organizational power or the power of the word, leave a personal imprint on society that the historian cannot ignore. Then all the details of a person's life assume special significance, and we have the need for biography, to tell us how this person was formed and why he acted as he did.

There is of course an infinite host of events making up the life of human society now and in the past that the historian cannot possibly deal with. He must leave this to the social scientists, who can then present him with conclusions concerning the relevant conditions of life, beliefs, relationships, and forms of behavior common to large numbers of people. The historian considers these particular generalizations together with the outstandingly significant individuals and events that have helped give society the form shown by these generalizations. For example, the particular fact that the Llewelyn Jones family in Bloomington, Indiana, moved into a house with inside plumbing in July, 1920, while very important to the individuals concerned, is devoid of historical significance; but when the Census Bureau adds up the total number of toilets in the country as a whole and publishes figures showing the decade-by-decade increase in the percentage of families enjoying such convenience, we have a significant, generalized fact of social history.

Some particular facts, insignificant in themselves, are of historical interest because they are representative of a large number of similar facts that help to make up an historical way of life. Thus the Shelburne Museum in Vermont is an important monument of social history because its buildings and artifacts are examples of the mode of life in New England a century or more ago. If the items in the museum were neither typical nor influential, they would be mere curiosities, and the historian would look elsewhere for meaningful material.

Sometimes we find that a certain activity can be historical in one epoch and routine in another. At one time it may be an innovation, a unique step that sets the pattern and helps shape society, while later it is only a prosaic part of everyday life. Take, for example, such a matter as the keeping of government financial records, which was a crucial step in the development of national monarchies in the Middle Ages, but is now only a dull though complicated procedure taken for granted by everyone. In our own time we can see scientific research becoming routinized. A generation ago a major discovery was still an historic event and a remarkable individual achievement; now it is a "development" that is almost automatically ground out so long as governments and corporations provide the funds to keep their laboratories going.

We can say by way of summing up that there are two requirements for regarding a fact as historical. First, it must be particular, whether individual and concrete or general and abstract. Secondly, it must be socially significant, either by having a particular effect on society as a whole, or else, as a general conclusion or typical illustration, by reflecting the character of society as a whole.

Naturally the concrete and abstract particulars that make up history must be taken into account by the other social sciences. They in turn supply generalized conclusions to history, while history sets the specific context of unique times, places, and events that shape the whole life of society as the social sciences study it.

An historical approach may correct some of the interpretations of the other social sciences, as well as many popular notions, through its regard for specifics and its resistance to either-or over-simplifications. It is common, for instance, to hear of "Communist expansionism" as one great force operating everywhere all the time. Historically considered, however, with a view to specific times and places, Communist power successfully expanded in Europe only in 1945-1948 and in the Far East in 1945-1954. So far this is the extent of it, with the exception of Castro's Cuba in the 1960s. Reduced to specifics, the phenomenon of Communist success is somewhat less formidable than we at first tend to think and invites explanation in terms of specific reasons at specific times and places instead of the mysterious push of an abstract "ism" such as "expansionism." As this example suggests, the uniqueness that history deals with is a fundamental characteristic of human affairs, and the other social sciences ignore it at their peril.

The Chronological Dimension

What separates history from every other kind of inquiry about human affairs is its fundamental concern with time—the before and after, cause and effect relationship of events. History views all human activity in the setting of particular times and sequences of events from one time to the next. It is therefore concerned more than the other social sciences with questions of change, or of repetition, or of continuity or development in society's affairs.

The time perspective accentuates history's concern with studying the unique characteristics of particular situations and events. One morning can never be the same as another, and every particular or general fact about society must be seen in its specific time setting and evaluated accordingly. Not only does the meaning of a fact or conclusion depend upon its date, but generalizations about facts must include the recognition of change over time. This is as true of the present as of any point in the past.

In the study of history, as well as in the other social sciences, there is a tendency to emphasize recent events, evidenced by the number of courses devoted to the more modern periods and the uneven allocation of time in individual history courses. There are good reasons for this. First of all, recent events are closer to the present and its problems, and have a more direct bearing on decisions affecting the future. The most recent events have personally involved every living adult, in one way or another, and this is added incentive to study them.

For the historian, recent events require more detailed attention because it is harder to judge and generalize about them. Faced with the complexity of our own times, we cannot tell which developments will have important consequences and which will not. It is easier for historians to summarize the historical significance of the whole Middle Ages than the twenty-year period between the two World Wars. Besides, the most recent events are being subjected to historical study for the first time, and therefore require the difficult work of organizing and interpreting the data into the first roughly intelligible explanation of what has been going on.

Secondly, the changing nature of society in recent generations has made history different in kind. Since the beginning of the Industrial Revolution two centuries ago, the complexity of society has increased enormously, and even the size of most countries has multiplied many times in the great modern population explosion. This has been the greatest change in the life of mankind since written records first made history possible. Progress has brought with it a fantastic growth in the number of events that have historical significance and a mountainous increase in the amount of written records that historians must explore in studying these events.

Finally, the spread of communications and political and economic links around the globe has brought about what we can truly call the unification of world history. Contemporary history cannot be confined to Europe or America, as most earlier historical study in the West was. Every part of the world is now involved in the critical flow of events. Even more, it has become necessary for Westerners not only to know recent events elsewhere in the world, but to look back in the past of strange civilizations to understand how this history, once ignored, now affects everyone's present.

The Integrated Study of Human Affairs

Since everything that exists in the past is history, and since everything we know is already in the past, all knowledge is in a way historical. As we have seen, history in its broadest sense includes the subject matter of all the other social sciences. The work of the humanities and natural sciences is also material for the historian, since it represents the past record of man's cultural, imaginative, and scientific achievements.

When history is divided into its various aspects or topics, we can see very clearly how it encompasses the other social sciences and the humanities. History pursues the backgrounds and roots not only of man's political experience, but also of his socioeconomic and cultural life. Dealing with all aspects in turn, it aims to demonstrate and explain the particular direction of civilization's development in relation to the unique historical context of each epoch. History would approach science, for instance, not to contrast past error with present truth, but to explain how scientific concepts were built up out of the efforts and experiments of each generation, and to show how particular lines of science were encouraged or impeded by the political, economic, or religious interests in particular times and places.

Because we cannot take one aspect of life in total isolation from its social setting, the study of history promotes a recognition of interrelationships. Generally speaking, historians oppose one-factor explanations, even if they concede that individual factors might loom larger at particular times. Aided by the generalized insights of the other social sciences, history tries to pull together its own recognition of the stream of unique and manifold events in time into a comprehensive view of the human experience.

History can be the keystone of the entire study of man. It is concerned not with one particular aspect of human activity, as the various social science and humanistic disciplines must be, but with all aspects, in all the complexity of their interrelatedness. History recognizes the reality of particular historic individuals and tries to understand their conduct and its consequences as much as the generalized movement of anonymous masses. After the other fields of inquiry have made their necessary, though artificial, distinctions between political, economic, social, religious, intellectual, and artistic man, the study of history restores unity to our understanding of mankind. It is this broad view of the individual and the particular as well as of the general and comprehensive that causes history to be recognized as one of the humanities as well as a social science.

Though it has not always managed to aim this high, history should ideally bring together and synthesize all the other realms of knowledge and their various analyses. History alone has the broad compass to see the true, complex interplay of motive, cause, chance, and circumstance in human life. To the historian falls the ultimate task of showing how virtue, vice, comedy, and tragedy form the drama of human existence.

4

HOW
TO STUDY
HISTORY

EVERY SOCIETY TAKES FOR GRANTED the importance of history. Every educational system requires that students study it. In undergraduate college instruction in the United States a year of European or American history is often mandatory. The reasons for this are obvious from the preceding chapters: some mature study of the past is vital for an understanding of the present and for a fuller appreciation of other studies.

Since history must be learned, the question is how to go about it. Learning depends upon interest, and interest depends upon how an individual grasps the significance or practical application or inherent excitement of a given subject. It is regrettably true that too often the student's experience with history misses all this and gives him only the numbing dullness of meaningless facts. This should not happen if the subject is taught and learned for the purposes we have been discussing—for the understanding of man, his past, present, and future; for the cultivation of one's mental powers; and for the sheer excitement of inquiry and discovery. Any learning that is not somehow related to these goals, but is forced along for its own sake, conveys only what Alfred North Whitehead condemned as "inert ideas," mental dead weight that can ruin the opportunity for genuine education.

Taking a Course in History

For many people the study of history begins and ends with formal school and college courses, too often a tedious ordeal, though this hardly need be so. What is a course, after all? It is an organized program of reading, listening, and talking about an important subject. The reasons for approaching history, like any other subject, through a formal course, are simple: it gives organization to the subject; it provides the discipline to stick at it week in and week out in order to master the material; and through the teacher it provides explanations

of difficult points and of any questions that the student does not understand.

Ordinarily the college history course is based on lectures (often supplemented by discussion sections); required reading assignments; and usually written assignments ranging from the book report to the research or term paper. The lectures are the core of the course; ideally the instructor uses them to set forth the broad patterns of his subject and to suggest explanations of cause and effect and significance. To some it may seem that the lecture only duplicates the reading and is an unnecessary holdover from the Middle Ages when, before the advent of printing, the scholar in effect dictated his book to his students as they took notes. Actually the lecture should supplement the printed text, by balancing the factual emphasis of the latter with a more interpretative approach. Furthermore, there is special pedagogical power in the direct personal presentation of ideas. Good lecturers can achieve an impact in the dramatization of their subject that has more impress on their students than even the best writing.

When attending a lecture, you should remember its interpretive purpose. Don't attempt to take verbatim notes on illustrative detail that is in the reading anyway; concentrate on the main ideas, with an effort to note the personal interpretation of the lecturer. It is worthwhile to go over your notes immediately after the lecture to establish firmer recall of the material, to add other points that you did not have time to write down, and to make a summary of the notes that accent the main points for future study and reference.

Reading assignments are designed to familiarize you with the essential facts and acquaint you with the supporting details. As the following sections will explain, you need not make yourself a slave to the reading, noting down everything and memorizing it. You should pick and choose, scan, and synthesize in your own mind. Notes are best made after reading a whole section or chapter, preferably as marginal notes in the book itself if you own it. Workbooks and study guides are helpful if you have not acquired the knack for analyzing and summarizing your reading, but they are crutches that you should ultimately be able to dispense with.

The discussion section—the group of perhaps ten to thirty students into which a lecture class may be divided once a week or so—has an often unrealized potential. It is a supervised opportunity to talk about history, which can be one of the most effective ways for the student to digest information and concepts and to explore the subject for new insights. To profit by the discussion class, you should regard it as an opportunity, not an inquisition. If the instructor keeps asking questions, it is doubtless because the students fail to speak up on their own. Go to the section meeting armed with questions and ideas that you have prepared beforehand. The instructor will welcome them. Don't be afraid to try out your opinions, to make mistakes, or to subject yourself to criticism. This is the way you learn. One of the purposes of discussion is to reveal students' misconceptions so that the instructor can correct them.

The discussion in a history course should be a real conversation among the students and the instructor, not a recitation by one student at a time in a sort of dialogue with the instructor. Accordingly, you should make a point of facing your co-students and speaking directly to them. For a good discussion, the round-table arrangement is much better than the conventional row-by-row of students all facing the teacher.

Talking in class discussion is good training in the enunciation and clear phrasing that are essential for effective oral communication in any situation. You will realize the importance of these skills if you take an interest in what the rest of the class has to say and try to follow the discussion. All too often you will find that students don't speak loudly and clearly enough to be understood, but the others are likely to sit stolidly back without complaining because they view the dialogue as a recitation by one student for the benefit of the teacher alone.

For anyone interested in history, at least one formal course at the college level is a must to get started with the right approach. A good course is a multiple learning experience. Eye, ear, tongue, and pen are all called into play as avenues to the mind, and all are in turn being trained as they are exercised in the pursuit of historical knowledge and understanding.

Facts and Significance

The purpose of history courses is not encyclopedic factual knowledge, but understanding and an ability to think historically. History cannot be taught or learned, like mathematics or elementary foreign language, as a cut and dried sequence of information and principles to be memorized step by step. As the previous chapters have attempted to show, the study of history means acquiring the ability to think imaginatively, to organize information, and to use facts in order to discover and appreciate significant ideas.

In part, the familiar emphasis on the rote learning of facts is due to the examination system. We require an exact rating of a student's attainment. The teacher with hundreds of students, or the College Board examiner with hundreds of thousands, needs some quick and "objective" way of evaluating the papers before him, so he chooses the true-false or multiple-choice type of question that, if not well phrased, may accentuate the unrelated fact. Since the exam cannot cover everything that the student knows or should know, it becomes a spot check, where randomly selected questions are used to sample the student's store of factual knowledge. For the student the main problem is, then, to anticipate what will actually be sampled, and he tries to second-guess the examiner. Unfortunately, some teachers may in response try to outwit the student by posing the most obscure and unlikely questions. As a result, the whole teaching process is undermined: instead of telling the student what he should know, and why, the teacher tries to outfox him and keep him in the dark. The students come back with, "What are we responsible for?," and the teacher is likely to answer, "Everything in the textbook." The students cram to memorize every conceivable unconnected detail that might come up in a true-false or "identification" question. They regurgitate on the exam, get a grade (often machine-graded), and sometimes don't even learn which questions they missed or why. In fact, they don't care; the healthiest thing in this situation is the speed with which students cleanse their minds of the awful intellectual conglomeration with which they have stuffed themselves, and forget the entire meaningless substance of the course.

The foregoing is perhaps a caricature of most college teaching of history—though by no means of the high schools —but enough of it creeps into college-level teaching and examining to make it a real problem. It can never be emphasized enough that real learning is not simply a matter of memory, but of interest and understanding. If memorization is put first, it will kill interest and deaden understanding. But if the latter are carefully cultivated, memory will take care of itself. In short, a person should never try to memorize a fact if he doesn't know its significance; and if he understands its significance, it is almost impossible to forget the fact.

This being the case, why should history deal with factual details at all? Without detail, events and ideas are lifeless and meaningless. Think of the Civil War buff who, as a hobby, studies the battles in great detail—his interest in the subject has made the details interesting, and his acquaintance with them makes the subject interesting. Similarly, the student should become acquainted with some details—about the life of

Napoleon, for instance, or of Lincoln—not in order to memorize each fact, but simply to discover the man as a flesh-and-blood person. The details are to be read or surveyed for the purpose of understanding; they are not to be learned by rote just because they are in the textbook.

Every important historical fact—Napoleon's seizure of power on 18 Brumaire, for example—has to be cemented into the student's understanding from two directions. From above, it must be tied into a conception of a broad pattern or trend—for the present example, the French Revolution and its stages, culminating in a nationalistic dictatorship. From below, the fact must be supported by acquaintance with the tangible historical details—for instance, Lucien Bonaparte stalling the Council of Five Hundred while his brother was getting his courage up for the coup d'état—that impress the rather abstract event as a living thing in the memory. The same goes for Lincoln's election in 1860, as the culmination of a trend (the sectional crisis over slavery), and as a statement embracing some vital details (Lincoln's antislavery speeches, the split in the Democratic party, the commitment to secession which Lincoln's victory precipitated in the southern states).

The teacher and the learner should distinguish among several different types of historical information that ought to be mastered. There are major facts—the existence of key individuals, events, institutions, movements, and concepts—that should be readily available in the student's mind so that he can bring them into an essay, or write a page of detail on each when called upon to do so. Who can talk of the history of Modern Europe if he cannot do this with such "facts" as the French Revolution, Robespierre, the Estates General, the Rights of Man? There are lesser, more concrete facts—individuals, events, and geographical places—that are nevertheless part of the vocabulary, the mental furniture of any educated person, and the student should be able to identify them if necessary. The word of caution here is that the student should be explicitly taught which points of detail are important enough to be so learned, and why they are important—what their significance is. Better yet, the student should learn in the course of a year or two of college work in history how to judge for himself which details are memorable in this sense and which are in the reading just to be experienced as supporting color. Finally, he must be taught—or must learn for himself—how to see the broad outlines of a subject. He must learn how to use the conceptual framework of history; he must recognize the diversity and classification of human experience according to periods, places, and aspects; and he must be aware of all the various social institutions and movements. With this we emerge from the welter of factual learning, which is essential but secondary, and approach the true ends of historical study—a capacity to reason historically and a comprehension of the historical nature of man.

Generalization and Detail

So far we have assumed that a fact is a fact, a kind of solid atom of historical information that is piled up with thousands of others to produce a significant pattern or generalization. In truth there is no sharp line between facts and generalizations— all individual "facts" are really generalizations that embrace many lesser facts. The student is asked to identify Robespierre.

Is Robespierre a "fact"? Or does his name actually represent a generalization about the myriad facts of his personal biography and his public career right up to the guillotine?

Every fact of history is a statement about a whole set of items of space, time, and matter. Thought about history would be totally impossible were it not for the generalizations that group infinite bits of information into simple notions that the mind can work with. All learning of history is learning about generalizations—how to form them, how to understand and remember them, how to use them to arrive at new ideas and new generalizations.

Generalizations and facts must go together—generalizations giving relevance to facts, facts giving life to generalizations. If the student's mind is filled with mere facts, he cannot see the forest for the trees. If he knows only generalizations, he cannot see the trees for the forest.

Generalizations do not have to be vague. They can be definite and meaningful, or they can be indefinite and meaningless. To say, as students frequently will, that on the eve of the French Revolution "the people were dissatisfied with their unfair conditions" is vague. Equally brief and general, but far more meaningful, is the statement, "The middle class and peasants resented the privileges of the nobility."

Historical generalizations may be infinitely varied, from the very limited to the very broad. Limited generalizations organize the details of historical observation into what are usually recognized as "facts"—the formation of the Committee of Public Safety, the Reign of Terror, the coup d'état of 9 Thermidor. Broad generalizations attempt to map out the great currents and motive forces of history. These may be simple notions, such as "the rise of democracy" or "Western civilization," or very complicated ideas, such as Marx's theory of class struggle or Pareto's theory of the circulation of élites. In between are the generalizations that arrange individuals, places, and events into ideas, such as "the Third Estate," "the economic causes of the French Revolution," "anticlericalism," "the Great Fear."

Intermediate generalizations really give more meaning to the study of history than do either the limited or the broad ones. They are the true building blocks of historical understanding. Without them the small points are meaningless and unlearnable, and the broad ones are baseless and inapplicable. Intermediate generalizations are the nub of the historian's work, where he must combine facts and imagination to fashion the record of the past into concepts that are both meaningful and reliable.

The work of constructing generalizations is never done, because, as with art, the work is imaginative and hence subjective. Inevitably, an historian is going to be influenced by his own times and his own point of view in the way he sets up generalizations to organize and explain the past. Just as inevitably, later historians are going to see the past differently and revise their generalizations accordingly. The anticlerical historians of the eighteenth century, for instance, represented the "Renaissance" as a true rebirth of the light of learning after the Dark Ages; later historians argued instead that the Renaissance was merely a change of emphasis from religious to secular interests. Unfortunately there is a lag in transmitting the new views of historians to the general public, and American high school students still come to college believing the eighteenth-century generalizations about the Renaissance.

Closely related to generalizations are concepts, which are especially important in making sense out of the study of history. Concepts may be defined as fairly broad generalizations that attempt to explain details—such as the concept of the "Enlightenment" to explain what numerous Frenchmen wrote in the eighteenth century, or the concept of "class struggle" to explain why the French fought each other in the nineteenth century. Very little has been written to help the student learn to think conceptually; this is either taken for granted or approached indirectly. (One of the few books that attempt to explain directly what historical concepts are is the exciting and thoughtful work by Carl Gustafson, *A Preface to History*.)

There are of course pitfalls in learning concepts. Since they are the work of some historian's imagination, they must always be subject to question and revision. They must be supported by factual knowledge. Both teacher and student must remain aware that concepts are abstractions and that simply memorizing them is as fruitless as memorizing fragmentary details.

Another problem is that the ability to handle concepts and to grasp them in relation to the details varies tremendously from one person to another. Conceptual thinking is a particular gift—it can be trained, but native ability is vital. It also depends upon the individual's maturity, and it may not fully develop until a person is well along in his college years. Therefore the presentation of concepts must be very carefully gauged to the student's ability and stage of intellectual growth. The most common mistake is to give students too much conceptual material too soon, especially in high school, and then not enough later on.

This trouble stems in part from the way beginning history courses are usually set up. Concepts and generalizations are needed more, obviously, in the study of a very broad span of history than in that of a narrow period or particular country. High school and introductory college courses are usually of the very broad, survey type that requires the most generalization in order to cover the material and reduce the detail to intelligible and significant units. Thus, paradoxically, the introductory history survey is conceptually the most difficult. Advanced college courses, dealing with individual countries, periods, or topics, can give much more attention to the real-life details within their compass and come down to a much more basic level of generalization and concept. In terms of their intellectual demands on the student in this respect, the advanced courses are the easiest. Is this to say that the survey course should be abolished, or given last to college seniors? Not at all, for one thing that the survey offers is of vital importance at an early stage—the broad picture establishing the context and showing the relevance of further and more specialized study. The specialty has to be approached in such a framework or it makes no sense.

Survey and Depth

How do we emerge from the impasse where the specialized study of history makes no sense without a general framework, but where the general framework is itself too abstract and difficult for the beginning student to master? The answer is that

neither can be approached alone or understood all at once. Both must be attempted simultaneously, or in alternation, so that they constantly contribute meaning to each other.

Begin by getting the quickest, simplest bird's-eye view— the outline of a course or the table of contents of a particular book. Then look for the main subordinate points—the intermediate generalizations, perhaps, that give substance to the over-all picture. Make a time chart that shows you the basic chronology. Next, look into some details—not all of them, nor necessarily the first ones, but the details that bear on the most interesting or significant part of the whole. Read the details, not to learn them, but to become acquainted with them, to experience them in relation to the more significant abstractions. Where possible, form questions about cause, effect, and significance, and look for the details that help answer these questions. Give your curiosity free rein.

In this manner you can work through a subject layer by layer, so to speak, rather than binding yourself to follow history chronologically. As you dig down into more detailed and complicated layers, the broad and intermediate generalizations that you started with will be given more life and meaning.

Suppose again that you are studying a chapter on the French Revolution. You want first to note how the subheadings split the topic into periods, and to see what distinctive forces, leaders, and events they emphasize. Perhaps the first section is called "The Third Estate and the Constitutional Revolution." You immediately look for details that define these two concepts, without yet bothering to learn the more minute details of the debates and the sequence of crises. You search out what you need to know in order to answer general questions—why, for instance, did the constitutional experiment fail? Was it the death of Mirabeau or the personality of the king, the discontent of the Paris workers or the agitation of the Jacobins? Whatever the answer—and historians do not agree —you will have familiarized yourself with a variety of important facts in a way that makes them meaningful and not easily forgotten.

From time to time, you should look back at the over-all picture. What were the stages of the French Revolution and how did one lead to the next? How were the forces in each stage generated by the earlier history of France? What future strengths and weaknesses of the nation were rooted in each stage of the Revolution? If you proceed from the details back to the general concepts, you will see the latter in a new and more realistic light. And you will be learning and understanding history at the same time.

There are limits of time and human energy in the use of this method of survey and depth study. In most historical study there is no end to the little concrete details that can be studied to shed light on the larger details and generalizations. The total known detail of human history is astronomical, overflowing vast libraries. It is humanly impossible to master, or even to experience, anything but a small sample of it. Historians can and do spend lifetimes studying and researching just one period in the history of a single country. No wonder, then, that the poor freshman, confronted with the entire history of Western civilization in a one-year course, sometimes feels overwhelmed by it all.

Again there is an answer to this problem. Although the subject matter of history is composed of layers of generalization underlain by an almost infinite depth of detail, it is possible to cover any subject, broad or narrow, in any given amount of time. One can enumerate the main trends of all of Western civilization in five minutes or devote an entire course to the French Revolution alone. It is time and interest that set the limits to any project, and study must come to a halt after reasonable achievement in the available time.

This means that for the most part you have to be content with a still rather abstract picture of your historical subject—you haven't had time to dig down into the lower, more concrete, multifarious, and time-consuming levels of detail. On the other hand, to rest simply with this will leave you with a misleading, over-simplified view of the true nature of history. To correct this, it is highly desirable to spend part of the time in any course, whether survey or specialty, in a detailed, in-depth case study.

The value of the case study is to give you some experience with the living, bedrock details of history, even though you do not have time to work at this level through more than a small area of your subject. This is why the research or term paper is a valuable adjunct to any history course. (For the same reason, the deeply researched doctoral dissertation is an important intellectual investment in the training of the historical expert.) In researching for a case study you learn how people really behaved in a given event. From this you can imagine how they probably behaved in other circumstances, and thus develop a general view of the people, the places, the times, and the society or societies involved.

Organizing Historical Knowledge

Since history cannot be learned or understood all at once, not even in specialized courses, it must be organized and mapped out to expose it to meaningful study. This means recognizing the natural units through which it may be studied, one by one, and the relationships among those units. There are at least three important procedures for organizing historical information: *classification*, *linkage*, and *balance*. All are ways to tie

facts together into meaningful units, and all three must be used together to arrive at satisfactory comprehension of a given subject.

The principle of *classification* involves the division of historical data—both details and generalizations—into natural units of study. These are the pigeonholes in which historical information is stored while the mind is digesting and interpreting it. The classifications may be of three sorts, corresponding to the three dimensions of historical study—*chronological, geographical,* or *topical.*

The most obvious type of classification in history is *chronological*—ordering information by time sequence and dividing it up into periods. These units may be long or short, depending on whether the student is a surveyor or a specialist, but they should be based upon and marked off by important events and developments. Another obvious form of classification, equally pertinent to history and the other social sciences, is *geographical*—the classification of historical data according to the civilization, country, or other territorial unit in which they occur.

The third historical dimension is represented by classification according to *topics* or *aspects* of history—political, diplomatic, military, social, economic, cultural, religious, and so on. These divisions are important not only to permit specialized attention to one aspect of life, but also to organize the story of, let us say, one country in one brief period so that the student can grasp some of its complexity.

There are certain natural ways in which the principles of classification should be applied in teaching and study. If the chronological span of study is very long—the history of Western civilization, for example—the first principle to use is chronological, in order to break down the over-all span into more meaningful and manageable periods. If the chronological span is short but the geographical coverage very wide—the history of the contemporary world since 1918, for instance—it is necessary to apply the geographical classification and follow separately the development of each major region or country. The topical approach may be used at any time, but it is most appropriate when both the chronological and geographical limits of the subject are restricted, as in studying one country in a brief period. Within a particular topic, a further subclassification might best be made chronologically, such as a study of the sequence of new ideas in the intellectual history of eighteenth-century France or the economic problems of twentieth-century Britain. There are no absolute rules of procedure. You need to become something of an historical artist yourself to advance your understanding, but you must know the forms and colors that are available to you in composing your own canvas.

Historical classifications, while essential to learning, may run the risk of distortion by artificially slicing up the intricate fabric of the past, unless they are knit back together by appropriate linkages. This requires the recognition of logical and factual connections between the various natural segments of history: chronological, geographical, or topical. Linkage may work either backward or forward, to establish origins and causes or consequences and significance. It may seek to establish parallels or interrelations between the histories of different places or between different aspects of life at the same time. Diplomacy and war very definitely link the affairs of different countries, so much so that diplomatic history cannot easily be broken down geographically. But even in political history, which is usually studied country by country, a great deal of significance can be brought out by using the comparative method. For example, it is interesting to compare the monarchies of eighteenth-century France, Prussia, Russia, and Britain, to observe both the similarities and the differences, and perhaps to arrive at some generalizations about "enlightened despotism." Parallel time charts of events in different countries and on various aspects of history will greatly facilitate this sort of study.

Along with the analysis represented by classification and the synthesis represented by linkage goes the principle of *balance*, which is a measure of caution not to neglect an area of significance within the chosen realm of historical study. Balance applies to all the types of classification and linkage. Chronologically, it calls for due regard to each time period and to the need for more detailed attention to more recent periods that are better known but harder to generalize about. Geographically, it demands due recognition of different civilizations, of the various countries within a civilization, and of the regional differences of historical experience within a given country. Most important of all is the need for balance among the various aspects of historical study, to assure the comprehensive view that only the historical approach can offer. Traditionally, up to the late nineteenth century, history was concerned almost exclusively with politics and diplomacy. Not only were all other facets of experience neglected, but their possible influence on the political aspect was sadly overlooked. A balanced view of the different aspects of history in their complex interrelationship through time is basic to the student who wants to move on to the exciting questions of historical explanation. Fortunately, modern historical teaching and scholarship grant him full opportunity for this.

5

WRITING
ABOUT
HISTORY

THERE ARE TWO WAYS of defining what is meant by "history." It may be taken to mean the sum total of what has happened in the human past, or it may be understood more specifically as the written record of the past. In practice, virtually all that is known of history depends on the written record anyway, except for the auxiliary knowledge derived from archaeology and the interesting, though unreliable, oral traditions of folklore. As the written record of the past, the study of history is as much a literary subject as is the study of English. Ideally, every history course should include expository writing as a vehicle of clear thinking, and the experience of reading history purely as a form of literary art. Reading and writing, as training in thought and understanding, will remain the foundations of education as long as civilization endures.

Types of Historical Writing

Historical writing, like history itself, is a vast and varied subject. It has gone on in every society and every age since the dawn of civilization, though with accelerating quantity and complexity. And there is a variety of purposes that must be served by different kinds of historical writing.

Historical writing is, first of all, the production of records as part of the events themselves. These first-hand documents —the writings and utterances of leaders; the notes of eye witnesses; the letters, diaries, and recollections of participants; the dispatches by journalists for readers who want to know immediately what is going on—are the primary sources of history. Next come the efforts to compile and systematize the record in chronicles and yearbooks, followed by the books and articles written on the basis of intensive research to find out how and why events happened as they did. These, along with the great multivolume works of narrative history (a form popular in the ninteenth century, but, with a few exceptions, too demanding of money and patience for the twentieth), constitute the secondary sources. Finally, there are works written specifically for reference or instructional purposes—encyclopedia articles, handbooks, and textbooks—whose purpose is to draw from the record in order to present a clear and convenient (if oversimplified) picture to the learner. These are the tertiary, or third-hand, sources—useful, but hardly the final word. No student will have a reasonable appreciation of a given segment of history if he does not read a few secondary works of research and have at least some contact with primary source material.

So far as the student's writing is concerned, there are other established forms and purposes. Writing is an exercise in thinking—in organizing information, in relating details to generalizations, in combining ideas into a logical demonstration or interpretation. The most common form is the essay examination question, where the student must write at length on a given point. He must show not only what he remembers, but also his ability to decide what facts are relevant and to arrange them in a properly organized fashion. Book reviews are another common instructional device, as well as an essential medium of communication among professional writers and historians; their purpose for the student is to direct his attention to a work of historical research or interpretation and to test his understanding of it. Much more demanding is the assignment known as the term or research paper, where the student himself is required to execute a project of historical research, using both primary and secondary sources. In the term paper are found what are perhaps the greatest values of historical instruction: detailed study of the facts in a given case, careful organization, and reflective interpretation.

The Structure of Writing and Thought

One of the main differences between speaking and writing is the far more extensive and complex organization of ideas and information that is possible when words are put down on paper. This is why writing usually seems more of a challenge and a task, and also why extended papers or essays are important to provide exercise for the intellectual powers. But written work in history can be made reasonably simple if you become aware of the way in which an historical narrative is organized.

The principle is very much that of an outline, with its points, subpoints, and sub-subpoints. It is, in essence, the system of hierarchical relationship between generalizations and details set forth in the previous chapter. This requires every detail and every idea to be incorporated into some larger, reasonable proposition, leading to the central thesis that sums up the meaning of a chapter, an article, or even an entire book.

Our familiar units of grammar are the building blocks with which a meaningful structure of thought is constructed. Sentences, each conveying a definite idea, fact, or set of details, are combined to form a paragraph, which is nothing more than the extended statement of a certain point with mention of several pertinent aspects or details. It is essential that the paragraph have coherence, which is accomplished by a "topic sentence" (usually at the beginning) that states the point and provides a peg on which to hang the details of the rest of the paragraph. For example, in this paragraph the central point was stated in the first sentence (about grammatical units as building blocks), and the following sentences spelled the point out by showing how sentence units are put together to form a paragraph.

On a larger scale, paragraphs are put together into an extended discussion or section of a work, sometimes (as in this book) indicated by section headings or subheadings. Sections, in turn, make up a chapter, and chapters make up a book. But the principle of the topic sentence must be observed regularly throughout, so that there is always a nearby reminder of the objective of the details and ideas being presented. A section should have an introductory and a concluding paragraph, or else begin and end with careful wording that accomplishes the same purpose of telling the reader what he should look for and then reminding him of the significance of what he has just read. A work or portion of a work is invariably clearer if it has appropriate introductory and concluding sections. Above all remember that a statement must be tied into the rest of the account in a meaningful way. One sentence, except in conversation or journalism, can almost never constitute a paragraph by itself; it must be tied to some more general idea. A paragraph cannot be inserted into an account without a logical relation to what goes before and after it. A section or chapter that has no clear relation to the rest of the work had best be left out altogether; it only disrupts your organization and flow of thought.

If an historical account is prepared with these organizational points in mind—the subordination of details to larger points, a proper introduction and conclusion, the necessary logical linkage of one paragraph to the next and of one section to the next—the writer will be well guarded against the most common difficulty in historical discourse. This is the old forest and trees problem, where the writer can't see the general point because he is lost among unorganized details, or (less commonly) when he is overwhelmed by generalities and fails to spell out the details that will give his account concrete historical meaning. Both facts and their organization and interpretation must be brought out in proper balance, and systematic organization of thought and writing is the only way to accomplish this.

So far we have not spoken of the particular kinds of sections and points around which an historical narrative may be organized. Basically they are the same classifications of historical experience that we have employed in earlier chapters —chronological, geographical, and topical. Most of the time an historical narrative will be organized chronologically, with the sections determined by the important happenings. (Sections should not be set up on the basis of arbitrary calendar units, such as months, years, or centuries—this would be a chronicle, not a history, and would obscure rather than underscore the significance of the events.) On occasion it is perfectly proper for the writer to backtrack in his narrative and pick up the stream of events in another place (the geographical dimension) or in another aspect (the topical dimension). As we noted in Chapter 2, it is more meaningful to work first with geographical or topical distinctions if the over-all time span is short. In any case, the writer must try to discover which use and combination of chronological, geographical, or topical sections is most appropriate to his subject. There are no hard and fast rules; when he begins to organize, the historian has to work with the intuition of an artist, and to that extent his efforts become an individual work of art.

Pitfalls of Expression and Concept

The artistic requirements of history appear not only in the intuition necessary for good organization and interpretation, but even more in the verbal expression of a narrative. History is a form of literature, a discipline that depends on the accurate and effective choice of words to develop its content and conclusions. A primary task for the student is to learn how to master words, both general vocabulary and the special terminology of history, and to make them serve his own purposes.

There are good and bad ways to say anything. It is possible to write in a manner that suggests that you have a good grasp of a topic and have not just discovered it. Don't say: "In 1789 a revolution began in France." This insults the intelligence of the reader and makes him wonder about your own. Try to make use of the passing allusion that gently reminds the reader of your knowledge and insures his own. Thus: "When the French Revolution began in 1789, the middle class started to acquire political power." Notice that we didn't say "came to the fore," which is the sort of stale expression that should be avoided at all cost.

A more serious problem is outright misunderstanding of the meanings of words or the use of a wrong word that the writer has confused with another. The trouble here is partly inadequate experience in English composition and partly the nature of the language itself. Most of the specialized and abstract words in English have been formed by putting word roots from French, Latin, or Greek into polysyllabic compounds. Contrary to German or Russian, which make their compounds out of their own roots, the usual English of conversation offers no clue as to the meaning of the foreign-derived compounds, which have to be learned as entirely new words. To make matters worse, the stress in the English compound is usually in the wrong place, not on the syllable that carries the most meaning. The result is that English-speaking students invariably confuse different words that sound alike. They will say "refute" when they mean "reject," and "delegated" when they mean "relegated." "Instigate" is used so often to mean "institute" or "initiate" that the error has almost produced a change in the standard language. With more logic than grammar, intransitive verbs will be used with a transitive meaning —I have found "culminate" meaning to complete or to consummate, and "dwindle" meaning to reduce. Throughout, the problem is that the student does not hear these words in conversation and is probably not attentive to their exact sense when he reads them. He must therefore try to develop his word sense by constant awareness of meanings when he reads, writes, listens, and speaks.

Along with the misuse of words, vagueness is a chronic problem. Both difficulties are less the fault of the student than of instruction that tries to push him too fast into too much abstraction, before he really understands what he is talking about. Students feel a pressure to use very general terms, such as "stabilize" or "evolve," without stopping to realize specifically what was going on in the history they are discussing. Often they discover that they can get away with general statements (best known as "bull") that disguise their own actual ignorance. "The political situation declined," one student wrote of pre-revolutionary Russia. Whatever he meant, he said very little. Almost always it is possible to take such a statement, and, without making it any longer, substitute concrete terms that greatly enhance its meaning: "Most people refused to support the government" or "Power was given to more and more incompetent ministers."

Apart from these problems of good writing, there is another area of difficulty in historical discourse that is even harder to deal with, because it involves the over-all understanding of the subject itself. This is the misunderstanding and misuse of historical terms and concepts. For instance, "feudalism" will be used to describe any system of landlords and peasants, instead of the decentralized system of hereditary government that it strictly denotes. "Democracy" will be applied to eighteenth-century English government, which, while representative, nonetheless represented only a narrow oligarchy and was anything but democratic. The "Renaissance" will be understood literally as a "rebirth" after the "Dark Ages" instead of a mere quickening and change of cultural style after the very impressive development of civilization in the "High Middle Ages." In each instance, the problem is as much unlearning as learning—unlearning a vague, popular, or high-school meaning so that the mind is free to grasp the accurate, historical meaning.

The influence of the present on the understanding of the past is always an obstacle, even for the professional historian, so the novice deserves sympathy. He can't help looking at the past with today's standards of value and assumptions of motivation. He is always looking for economic motives and rational economic measures of accomplishment. He tries to interpret nationalism as a quest for economic "welfare"; he assumes that the bonds of serfdom somehow rested on "efficiency." It is less forgivable perhaps to imagine that present conditions of economic potential, social structure, or communication prevailed in the past. But all of these mistakes are natural, and only assure the teacher's challenge and opportunity: to recognize the way his students tend to think and then to widen their horizons, to give them a new awareness of the variety and potential of human experience. It is up to the teacher to catch and correct such fumbling crudities as "the people thought . . ." and to train his students to the level of thinking of which they are capable. This might, of course, deprive us of some interesting remarks. "After the corn laws were passed," one student wrote on an exam, "the people were miserable. They were finally done away with."

History as Literature

History is written to be read. It is a form of literature in every sense of the word, and therefore is subject to the standards of literary criticism—the writing may be good or bad, and the reader can quickly judge which. History involves the imaginative understanding of experience and its communication to an audience. It is closely related to the art of the novel, for both tell a story, the main difference lying in the amount of imaginative reconstruction of facts and personalities. History is drama—the most truly dramatic kind of human experience, and often the inspiration for the greatest dramas in the literal, theatrical sense.

The literary value of history depends on the particular kind of writing. Textbooks, which are aimed at the student to tell him what he should know, are notorious for their bad style and dull approach. Articles and monographs, works that are the direct result of specialized research, are also very often tedious and uninspiring, except to the expert who needs to know the results of new inquiry in his particular field.

The best historical writing is usually found somewhere in between, in the book that takes a large or significant subject and tells what happened. Such a book—Garrett Mattingly's *The Armada*, for instance, or Georges Lefebvre's *The Coming of the French Revolution*, or Bruce Catton's three-volume series on the American Civil War—is inherently more interesting. This is the only kind of historical work that is apt to appeal to a noncaptive readership and have a chance to reach the nonfiction bestseller lists. Students are always pleasantly surprised when they encounter this kind of book (frequently authored by a nonacademic historian). For example, a freshman class assigned to read Alan Bullock's *Hitler* reported that it had "color," was "not dry," "not a pile of facts," that you could "see what the person is really like," and that they appreciated some "speculation." The secret is that this kind of work develops its subject with the proper use of descriptive and explanatory detail, which is not meant to be learned, but only to give life, color, interest, and added meaning to the narrative.

Just as there are—and must necessarily be—different kinds of historical writing for different purposes, so are there different kinds of reading required for different purposes. It is a far cry from perusing a novel to picking one's way through a philosophy or science text, and documents and newspapers will not be read in the same way as a basic history of a strange civilization.

As many as five different levels of intensity in reading can be distinguished. The midpoint is normal rapid reading to follow the story line, as you would read a novel or a history like *The Armada*. More intensive is careful reading necessary to follow an argument or demonstration, as I hope you are reading this book. Most intensive (and often overdone) is the study of a textbook to learn its essential contents, usually with notetaking, rereading, and reflection. In the other direction, it is possible to scan a passage or even a whole book to get a quick impression of its contents and approach. In a great deal of nonfiction, the reader will grasp and retain from this method just as much as he would by a careful reading, and in far less time. Finally, there is skimming—the quick search through a document or book to find particular points that the reader is looking for. Skimming is particularly important in historical research, when the researcher has to sift through a large mass of material to pick out the points that are relevant to his subject.

One of the important objectives of historical instruction is to teach the student how to read, in the sense of using the proper method of reading for the particular subject and material. It is important to break the habit of reading everything or trying to learn everything between two covers. The book is a tool, and the reader must not be a slave to it. It is no crime to let part of a book go unread. On every subject there is vastly more in print than one person can handle, and the point is to learn how to select both the material to be read and the method of reading it. Only in this manner can the student open up for himself the avenue to true appreciation and enjoyment of that branch of literature which is the written record of the past.[1]

[1] Any book, text or otherwise, that has been important to your own educational development ought to be your personal and permanent possession, as a

tangible record of your progress and development. The practice of selling off one's old college textbooks is deplorable, as is the yearly recall, reuse, and eventual destruction of public school textbooks. Buy all the books you can, taking advantage of the vast choice available in paperback. The cost is small when you realize that once a book is yours, you can make repeated, convenient use of it and, more important, can mark and annotate it. I don't mean the helpless underlining with which many students fill their texts, but marginal notes and end-of-chapter summaries that will recall what you have read and thought far better than any notebook. Meanwhile, make long-term plans for a good library of your own—the surest mark of an educated person.

6

HISTORICAL
RESEARCH

THE BASIC DIFFERENCE between the creative literary artist and the historian is the source of the latter's material. It comes not from imagination and personal experience, but from study —the study of the written records of the past, in other words, historical research.

All narrative of events, all the sweeping generalizations of the textbooks, all historical understanding rest on the foundation of historical research. Research is necessary to find the evidence of past events; to sift, organize, and interpret the evidence; to show, as nearly as possible, what really happened—and how and why. Research is so important in history that some acquaintance with its nature and methods should be an integral part of the student's work, just as it is in the laboratory side of instruction in the natural sciences. It is particularly important in developing the qualities of mind— the breadth, skepticism, organization, and judgment—that historical training aims at.

Problems and Sources

The task of historical research is to discover the foundations of historical truth and understanding in the deep substrata of detail. Research goes to the primary sources of history, those records and writings produced in the course of the events themselves, and with them constructs or refines the intermediate concepts and generalizations that support or correct the simple, sweeping picture of history that the narrative survey presents. Did the French peasants resent the privileges of the nobility? Georges Lefebvre spent years researching provincial archives and land records in northern France to find out as exactly as he could whether this was so, and in what way, and for what reasons. Research of this nature is the ultimate way to resolve any question of historical truth or interpretation.

The scope of research is as vast and deep as the entire

subject of history. No human being has the time and energy to research more than a small segment of the total human record if he is to work with the thoroughness that reliable historical understanding requires. For the professional historian, no less than for the student, research has to be tackled one topic at a time in order to keep the effort both meaningful and manageable. The topic should arise from some broader question or problem that gives meaning to the research, which inquires into some aspect of the problem in an effort to explain or illustrate it. Research thus has a major role in the case study, which we have emphasized as the inquiry in depth needed to counterbalance the broad, superficial treatment in a textbook or lecture course.

Topics for research, be it an undergraduate term paper, a Master's thesis, or a scholarly book, can be marked out in any way that the researcher sees fit. Here again there is an artistic aspect, in choosing and defining the subject so that it makes sense and permits a coherent picture. Students frequently take topics that are too broad, because they do not realize the quantity and depth of available detail. It is educationally more valuable to narrow the topic, to sharpen the focus, and thus to permit more thorough research in the time at the student's disposal, provided of course that he keeps in mind the questions and broader issues that make the inquiry meaningful. If it is not linked to such broader points of significance, a narrow research topic may become a fit subject for ridicule—"Some Like It Hot: The Evolution of the Dijon Mustard Industry, 1812-1840."

A research topic should be approached in the manner recommended for any historical study—a general survey first, with the formulation of particular questions for inquiry, followed by progressively deeper probing. The secondary and tertiary sources should be used first to find out what the topic looks like in general and what other researchers have said about it. Only when the researcher has a good outline and some probing questions in mind is it economical for him to start spending much time with the primary sources. Here he is obliged to skim and select, gathering impressions and evidence that will help him answer or perhaps revise his leading questions.

The student who is new to research is likely to be overwhelmed by the amount of source material in any good library, and at the same time he may well miss some of the few books and articles that are indispensable for his particular topic. Fortunately there are a variety of aids that will greatly facilitate the work of locating sources, if only the student knows about them and gets some practice in their use. First and foremost is the library card catalogue, with its listings by subject as well as by author and title. The only caution here is in consulting subject classifications—a book may not have been classified under the particular heading you consult, or it may contain material on your topic even though it is mainly on a different subject. Once you have located your subject on the library shelves, it will pay to browse through the other books on the same or similar subjects.

To proceed more systematically you should learn how to use the library reference aids. There are bibliographies, some (like the *Guide to Historical Literature* published by The American Historical Association) sampling the whole of history and some giving an exhaustive list of books on particular countries or topics. A good beginning may be the bibliography or suggested reading list in your own textbook, while the secondary works you consult will give you invaluable specific help in their bibliographies and footnotes. One good source leads to another.

Important factual reference aids in any good library include, aside from the familiar dictionaries and encyclopedias, the *Encyclopedia of the Social Sciences*, the biographical directories (*Who's Who*, *Dictionary of American Biography*, *Dictionary of* [British] *National Biography*), statistical guides, and directories and handbooks for specific subject matter areas.

Some kinds of sources are harder to locate—articles in periodicals, pamphlets, government documents, and unpublished source materials, such as collections of letters and records. Here a session with the reference librarian—whose job is to help you—is a good idea, particularly because resources and arrangements vary from one library to another. Articles in English language periodicals are well indexed by author and subject in the triennial series *Reader's Guide to Periodical Literature* (for popular and news magazines) and the *International Index to Periodicals* (since 1965 the *Social Science and Humanities Index* for journals of scholarship). The *International Index* is often overlooked by students who have learned to use only the *Reader's Guide* in high school, but actually it is much more important for college work. There are many other specialized indexes; for history, you should know about the following: the *Essay and General Literature Index* (indexing the individual articles in multiauthor books), the index of the Public Affairs Information Service (giving both books and articles on history, social science, and public problems), and the series of *Historical Abstracts*, which gives thumbnail summaries of articles on every historical subject published anywhere in the world. Current news is conveniently tabulated in information services, such as *Facts on File* and *The New York Times Index*. A yearbook such as the British *Annual Register of the World's Events* or a good encyclopedia yearbook can also be very useful. To keep up to date on historical literature, get to know the quarterly journal of the American Historical Association, *The American Historical Review,* with its book reviews by professional historians and its listing of new articles country by country. The association also publishes, through its Service Center for Teachers of History, a very useful pamphlet series presenting new interpretations and bibliographies on the most significant historical topics.

How do you keep track of all the bibliography that is available to you, and how do you decide what to use? The answer lies in a simple record-keeping device—a file of 3 x 5 cards, one for each source that you consult. The bibliographical card file should become a permanent working habit of the student or researcher. Every notation of a source should immediately be written out on a 3 x 5 card. Never write out lists of books. Never jot down titles on the backs of old notebooks, for the information will simply be lost or have to be redone. Be ready to record new items; carry a supply of 3 x 5 cards when you go to class, to the instructor's office, or to the library. Write out a card for every title that you notice and may possibly be interested in, with full bibliographical data —author, title, publisher, place and date of publication, number of pages, and library call number (if you have looked at the book or the card catalogue). You may keep your card file arranged alphabetically by author, by topic, or both; although as you go on from one project or course to another, a subject division becomes natural. Never throw your cards away. Keep building your bibliographical file as long as you go on reading and writing, which ought to be your whole lifetime. Build the file not only for research projects, but also for general reading interests. You will accumulate an invaluable record of your efforts and discoveries.

To help you decide what to read and how to evaluate it, it is a good idea to put some information about the author and his approach right on each card. Try to identify the author, at least to the extent of his dates, nationality, specialty, and perhaps his party or viewpoint. This will be important in the process of critical evaluation discussed in the next section. If you have scanned the book, you may also want to jot down a summary of the book's contents, its thesis, and your opinion of the book's over-all merit or usefulness to your project. A convenient source for finding judgments about authors and books is the *Book Review Digest*, published annually, with its excerpts from actual book reviews. These points of information on your cards will help you decide which sources are the most important and most reliable, and which can be put aside for supplementary checking later on. Sources, like details, must be kept under control and made to serve you, or else you will be swamped.

Techniques of Research and Reporting

The experience of historical research can give you intensive training in how to think, if you survive the usual sink-or-swim assignment. Research is especially good in teaching a person how to find, sift, classify, and generalize about any kind of information. Certain procedures of this sort—on a par with test-tube washing in chemistry—have to be learned in order to do effective historical research, but they are invaluable in the long run to make complex tasks relatively easy and manageable. It would indeed be desirable to teach the methods of historical research and composition in a laboratory, where all the students would practice under the supervision of an instructor, though this is not a traditional arrangement outside the natural sciences and the creative arts.

The first imperative for research is an outline, to be prepared when you are beginning to collect information, not just when you start writing. The outline should serve to organize your topic according to the rules discussed in earlier chapters. It should embody the questions of significance that you are going to try to answer, and give you guidelines in the selection of relevant source material. It need not be elaborate, and it must not be rigid, but it must be reasonably concrete, including at least the first level of subtopics below your principal divisions. Don't hesitate to revise the outline as soon as the results of your research or writing make it desirable to do so.

The mechanical heart of your research operation is the file of content information, which is best kept on 5 x 8 file cards. (For course study notes and other records of a more general nature, the full-page format of a loose-leaf notebook is better.) Write notes, summaries, and quotations from your source reading directly on the card, taking care to note the source and page number so that you will not have to return to the source in order to write the footnote. Be careful to distinguish between your summary and a direct quotation; all too frequently a student will copy a passage onto his note card (perhaps with slight paraphrasing), leave out the quotation marks, and later write the passage into his term paper. Technically he has committed plagiarism, though he intended no deception and he footnotes the source.

For more extensive recording of information such as documents, statistics, and key articles, photocopiers and microfilm reader-printers have become universal labor-saving equipment. Every student should become acquainted with the value of these devices, though you must remember that data reproduced by these means is still subject to note making (like any other source) for the purpose of condensation, selection, and classification, before it is finally recast in your own words.

In taking notes, don't spare the cardboard. It is far better to take an excess of notes on a large number of cards than the contrary. Always use a fresh card for information from a new source. Do not put two unrelated points, even from the same source, on one card—you may want to file the points under different classifications. Don't write on the back of a card—it will at best be a nuisance and may well go unnoticed altogether. Remember that the function of the card file is to permit the reclassification of data after you have abstracted it from the sources, so that you can sort facts from each book or document into the various subject or chronological classifications that you have set up in your outline. Don't forget to take notes on your own ideas that occur to you while you are doing research; they may be just as valuable to you as information from your sources, and you can't depend on your memory. Put your thoughts concerning each point on separate cards and label them as such, just as you would do with source information.

Suppose you are writing a paper on Robespierre's role in the Reign of Terror, and the card catalogue has led you to the very appropriate book by J. M. Thompson, *Robespierre and the French Revolution.* On page 70 you read:

> The Committee of Public Safety of April 6, 1793, originally consisted of nine Jacobins, of whom two, Barère and Lindet, became permanent members. At the end of May it was increased temporarily to fourteen members; but again reduced to nine on July 10, when Danton was excluded. Robespierre was not added till July 27. Four additional members, including Carnot, brought the total up to twelve by September 6; and these were re-elected monthly until the fall of the Jacobin government ten months later.

What notes do you make? There are facts here about the Committee, about Barère and Lindet, about Danton and Carnot, and about Robespierre. What facts does your outline suggest that your project requires? Certainly the election of Robespierre to the Committee on July 27, 1793, is an important event that you will probably give a paragraph to. So you make out a card, possibly labelled "Robespierre—career," and you write the note, "7/27/93—elected to Com. of Publ. Safety (3

mos. after established)." The note is brief; it is entirely in
your own words; and it emphasizes a point of timing that may
be significant. Other cards might be used to record the creation of the Committee, the purge of Danton, and the date when
the Committee became fixed in its membership of twelve.
The rest of the passage is for your purposes trivial, and you
ignore it. There is nothing that needs to be quoted. All of
your cards are marked "Thompson—*Robespierre*, p. 70," and
are ready to be classified either by subject or by date. Then
you get the idea that Robespierre, coming late to the Committee, must have attained prominence as a spokesman for what
the other members already felt; you put this point on another
card, and bear the thought in mind while you look for corro-
borating information.

Writing up the results of your research should not be put
off too long. Don't wait until your research is "complete"—
you should always be ready to go back to the sources after
you have written a first draft, when your problems and ideas
have come more clearly into focus. It is not a bad idea to
write a first draft section by section, while you are still col-
lecting source information. If you have set up your subject
matter card file properly, you can write each section almost
directly from the cards, though usually a great deal of condensation, selecting, and summarizing will be in order as you
boil the contents of your file down into a written narrative.

This is the point at which to distinguish carefully between
your narrative summary of events and direct quotation from
your sources. Quotation is a very effective device, though it
must be used with care. The most common mistake is to quote
too much, especially from secondary sources. Never quote
a secondary writer just to carry your narrative along, but only
in a supplementary way if his language or ideas need to be
illustrated. On the other hand, quote primary sources liberally
for illustration, but don't let the quotes run too long or leave
them without your own comment. In quoting a full sentence
or more, be sure that you identify the speaker in some fashion
in your text (as well as in the footnote)—e.g., "The British
ambassador reported . . ." or "As a noted authority on the
Revolution explains. . . ." If you want to use a quotation that

your source has taken from another source, try to locate the original source. If you can't find it or if you can't read the original language, you may use the statement anyway, with a footnote that shows the nature of the source and its original location: "Lenin, speech of Sept. 22, 1920, to a conference of the Communist party, *Sochineniya* (Works), 2nd ed., XXV, 399, as quoted in Louis Fischer, *The Life of Lenin* (New York, 1964), p. 400."

Footnotes are the student's great bugbear, but needlessly so. Remember that their purpose is to let your reader know the source and authenticity of the statements in your narrative. If he will already know a fact or have no doubt about it—for example, that Robespierre was guillotined in July, 1794—it is common knowledge and needs no note. If the material is a quotation, a footnote is obligatory, as it is also for statistics and particular points of information found in a single document or source. In between, the writer must use some judgment as to where and when a note is needed.

Don't forget to footnote a particular idea or interpretation derived from a certain writer, even if you don't quote him. Where possible, consolidate notes. If all the particular facts in one paragraph come from one source, use just one note including the various page numbers. Sometimes when you are summarizing an episode that has been treated at length in several sources, it is desirable to list them all in one explanatory note, as, "For an extended treatment of this point, see the following works. . . ."

Each footnote should include enough information to make the source meaningful to the reader. The first citation of a work should give the author, title, place and date of publication (and publisher, if your paper doesn't have a bibliography), volume number (if any), and page(s). If the next note is the same source, just say "*Ibid.* ("in the same place"), p. 99," even if the note is on a following page. Subsequent references to the source should be abbreviated "Jones, *op cit.* ("in the work cited"), p. 101." (In some recent usage, the author's name and the page number are sufficient for a subsequent citation.) If you use more than one work by Jones anywhere in the paper, then identify the particular work by its title or an abbreviation. For articles in periodicals or multiauthor books, be sure to give the author and title of the article you are citing, as well as the editor and title of the publication in which it appears. Subsequent references to such a source can simply give the author of the article, as "Smith, *loc. cit.* ("in the place cited"), p. 22." A final tip—in writing the first draft of your paper, write the complete footnote into your text just below the line to which the note refers. Then you can forget about numbering for the time being, and the note will be next to its subject if you revise and reshuffle your pages.

When it comes to writing up your work, your task will be made easier and your results better if you regard everything you put down as tentative and improvable. Write fast, and try to express your natural stream of thought. If you can't think of a word, leave a blank for the time being. Don't worry about fancy words and style, at least the first time through. For anyone who is not an especially gifted writer, it is usually best if he keeps his writing simple.

Sometimes the student feels constrained because he is not writing for a real audience. Don't suppose that you are writing in order to tell the instructor something new (though you may indeed come up with some details or concepts that he has not had occasion to become familiar with). You must regard your work realistically, as apprenticeship or practice on a less ambitious level. Perhaps the best solution is to imagine that your paper will be printed in a journal to be read by your fellow students. In fact it would be a salutary development if students did print and read each other's history papers, as they often do with their creative writing efforts in campus literary magazines.

Always plan to do two complete drafts. In the first draft, write the body first, then the conclusion, and the introduction last. As your thoughts take shape, go back to your research and your outline; prepare to revise your theories, your organization, and perhaps even the entire set of questions that guided your research. For the second draft it may or may not be a good idea to work from your first text, with cutting, splicing, correcting, and reshuffling of material. (Incidentally, if you want to make one or two additions to a page, don't try to cut and paste or staple; just write out another sheet marked "insertion to page X" and mark an arrow on page X where the insertion goes. It will then be copied in on the final typescript.) If your revisions are substantial, it is easier in the long run to write a fresh text, a least for the sections you are changing the most. Finally, go over the second draft for the literary qualities of style, word choice, grammar, punctuation, and paragraph structure. This editorial work is much easier if you can compose at least the second draft on the typewriter. When all corrections are on the manuscript, then the final clean copy may be typed. Don't forget to proofread the final copy; better to correct it in ink than not at all. And make a carbon copy for yourself, especially if you don't expect the paper to be returned by the instructor. Never throw a paper away—it represents too much of your own work and self-education, and (like your textbooks) you should keep it for permanent interest and reference.

Objectivity, Conflict, and Bias

In the dual process of research and writing, the student encounters the most challenging problems in historical thought.

These are the problems of determining what is important or true amid the mass of often conflicting information, of judging what is accurate or inaccurate in the sources he reads, and of recognizing and regulating his own opinions and biases as well as those of his sources. The total challenge of historical truthfulness is formidable, and even the greatest historians fall short at times, but the effort to rise to the challenge can offer perhaps the greatest of all educational values to the student of human affairs.

Objectivity is of course essential in historical research. This does not mean giving up all your opinions and values—that would not be human. What objectivity means in practice is the ability to face the facts, whether you like them or not. It is particularly important in facing unfavorable facts about people or institutions that you have endorsed because you thought they represented your values. The notorious lack of objectivity among Communists, for instance, is due not to their professed revolutionary values, but to their unwillingness to admit that the Soviet Union and the other Communist governments have in certain respects deviated from those values.

Nationalistic biases work the same way when a writer is determined to prove that his country has always been good and justified in its actions. For example, an elementary school textbook published in Boston in 1904 explained the outbreak of the War of 1812 thus:

> The captains of the English warships kept stopping our merchant vessels and taking sailors off them. In this way the King of England had managed to get several thousand Americans and he made them help him fight his battles against the French. At last we could bear this no longer. We told the king that unless he stopped taking our sailors we would fight. He refused to stop and in the summer of 1812 Congress declared war.[1]

A Canadian textbook of the same vintage seems hardly to be talking about the same war:

[1] David H. Montgomery, *An Elementary American History.* Boston, 1904, p. 176.

When British vessels entered the United States ports it was very common for their sailors, induced by better pay, to desert. By pretending to be citizens of the United States they defeated legal action taken to compel them to return to their ships. Great Britain then took matters into her own hands, and authorized warships to search United States vessels on the high seas for these deserters and to take them by force. Such a course in the present day would be regarded as very offensive and a good cause for resentment, but at that time it was not contrary to international law.[2]

This kind of extreme partisanship is what led Voltaire to remark that "history is only a pack of tricks we play on the dead."

Historical study should help the student become aware of the sources of bias, in himself and his contemporaries no less than among the personages of history. Generally, it stems from a we–they view of the world, the identification of oneself with a particular group—usually a nation or a religion, though sometimes a social class or a political party. Such a bias can often be unconscious, as with the ethnocentric attitude which assumes that the way of life of one's own nation is the standard for judging all others, or with the uncritical acceptance of any line of tradition. Unconscious biases can be projected far back into the past, as in the attitude that hails the Crusaders' onslaught on the Moslems—even though the latter, objectively viewed, were the civilized victims of barbarian aggression.

Occasionally bias has led writers to commit deliberate frauds and forgeries, for example the infamous "protocols of the Elders of Zion" concocted in the early 1900s to serve the purposes of anti-Semitism, with untold cruelties resulting. More often it operates by simple distortion, exaggeration, and selection, so that the biased account or accusation usually is a half-truth (and therefore more difficult to deal with). Bias

---

[2] John B. Calkin, *A History of the Dominion of Canada.* Halifax, 1898, pp. 217-218. This and the preceding quote were taken from Frederick G. Hinett, "The Nationalization of History Exemplified by the History of the War of 1812," M.A. thesis, The University of Vermont, 1953, pp. 47, 59.

is perpetuated because most people are naturally gullible when it comes to reinforcing what they want to believe.

It is only natural to find bias rampant in the sources of historical information, primary as well as secondary. History is largely the record of human beings striving and fighting for immediate advantage, and not many people are prepared to give up that advantage if it is threatened by an objective view of past or contemporary events. Sometimes after students have been introduced to the use of primary sources and the intuitive factor in secondary sources, they jump to the conclusion that the first-hand materials are necessarily more reliable, more objective, or less colored. They have forgotten that the primary sources, produced in the heat of the event, are automatically biased. These sources have to be used, but they must be used with discriminating judgment by the researcher, who hopes that his work will be a closer approximation of the truth.

Perhaps even more inaccuracy comes from sheer error. There is the imperfection of eye-witness observation, such that two witnesses will hardly ever give exactly the same description of an event. (If they do, you can safely assume that one has copied from the other.) Secondary writers, for all their care, will always make mistakes—of interpretation, of memory, and then simple slips of the pen (plus typographical errors that occur after the book has been written). Even more common is the literary excess that makes a conjecture look like a fact or a reasoned conclusion, as, for example, when a Kremlinologist writes about the behind-the-scenes power struggles in Moscow as though he had personally bugged the Politburo's conference room. Conjecture is perfectly legitimate, in its place, but it must be labelled with the appropriate "perhaps" or "it seems." Weigh what you read with the same caution in mind.

The requirements of reasonable objectivity do not rule out individual interpretation and judgment. We have seen that such interpretation, of a personal and imaginative nature, is inherent in the historian's work of organizing the record into a meaningful pattern. Consequently, there is no final truth in matters of historical interpretation and explanation.

Each successive historian is likely to see the same topic differently, especially because of the changing problems and assumptions that he recognizes in the world around him.

It is disconcerting to a student who is beginning historical study in depth to find conflicts of viewpoints and even of fact among different sources. He soon learns to be skeptical of anything in print—so much so that he may decide that you can't believe anything you read. Matters need not be left here if good historical judgment is brought into play. Each source, primary or secondary, can be evaluated through the methods of "internal" or "external" criticism. The former weighs the document or book taken by itself. Is it consistent or self-contradictory? What opportunity did the author have to know what he says? What is clearly fact, and what seems to be conjecture? What probable interest or bias might the author be defending, and has he stated facts contrary to his bias? External criticism weighs the document or book in relation to other materials and to what is known about the subject in general. How does the document compare with earlier and later accounts? Is it contradicted by other facts that it does not mention or facts that became known only after it was written? Does it represent an honest attempt to interpret all the known data as you understand them? Do frequent errors cast doubt on the reliability of the source? These are the cautionary questions, whose purpose is not to demolish historical truth, but to refine it.

The necessary latitude for historical opinion does not mean that the interpretation of the past may be manipulated at will to serve a particular bias that will not stand honest scrutiny. There is a point where imagination leaves off and dishonesty begins. You cannot, as many students think, seize on any pleasant thesis you want and proceed to "prove" it. History requires the judicious combination of imagination and respect for the facts, with the prime objective of finding out what the truth is to the best of your knowledge and ability. Research is the source of truth, even though it is a truth that is only approximate and always subject to the challenging insights that may come from new study. The opportunities for meaningful historical inquiry can never be exhausted.

7

THE
INTERPRETATION
OF HISTORY

HISTORY, AS AN ORGANIZED ACCOUNT of the past, is the product of individual historians, each working from a personal viewpoint and applying his own imagination to reconstruct the human record. The significance that each historian develops out of the historical record is therefore a work of personal interpretation. It follows naturally that no final, fixed set of historical principles acceptable to everyone will ever be arrived at. The meaning of history is always in flux, always a matter of controversy, out of which, we may hope, new insights will continue to flow.

Issues in History

Among individual historians there have been a number of recurring controversies about the nature and meaning of history, with shifts in the prevailing fashion depending on time, place, and party. Some historians have stressed the formulation of generalizations and the search for historical laws. Others have insisted on the uniqueness of each historical fact and situation. Some have sought and propounded one basic factor, be it economic, geographical, spiritual, or whatever, as the fundamental determinant of the course of history. Others have argued the multiplicity of factors, or the role of accidents and human decisions in shaping the course of events. Some believe the main significance of history is to explain the present. Others have defended the pure knowledge of the past as a value in itself. Generalizing loosely, Anglo-American historiography has leaned to the second side in each of these issues—the uniqueness of the fact, the multiplicity of factors, and the intrinsic interest of the past—while continental European historiography has inclined to historical laws, determining factors, and the meaning of the past as the source of the present.

This latter, predominantly European view of the historical process goes by the name of *historicism*. Historicism views man's total social experience as an historical process, within which any aspect can only be understood historically, since it is conditioned by its particular historical setting and background. Judgments of the rightness or wrongness of an action or event, in this view, can only be made relative to the historical setting and period in which they occur.

Since the work of an historian is itself an historical event, conditioned by time and place, it follows that the significance and truth of history can only be relative. The historian is a product of his times, his culture, and his social circumstances. Since historical interpretations are the expressions of individual historians, they inevitably involve the assumptions and concerns characteristic of the particular time, place, and social group. Consequently, to one degree or another, historical conclusions and the truth of history are relative to the epoch and background of the historian.

Historical relativism has been a major concern in discussions of historical method in recent decades. From the standpoint of relativism, the problem of bias is inherent in all historical writing. Occasionally the extreme view is taken that no historical objectivity is possible at all, and therefore why bother. A more moderate version is that valid questions may be pursued from a particular viewpoint, but that later historians from different backgrounds may ask new questions and cast new light on the truth.

Laws and Tendencies

Historicism is closely associated with the effort to approach history as a science and to propose scientific explanations for historical events and developments. History would indeed be easy to understand if all events could be accounted for on the basis of a set of simple laws like Newton's laws in physics. Of course, natural laws do come into play—people are physically subject to the law of gravitation and biologically subject to the law of death. But in the actual historical situation there are so many complex and variable factors, so much of the unpredictable human element, that it is impossible to use the ordinary scientific notion of "law." There are no identical situations, only parallels; there are no laws, only tendencies; there is no inevitability, only likelihood. There are always opportunities and alternatives for purposeful human action, just as there are always conditions limiting what people can accomplish by their action.

Because history is so complex and unpredictable, philosophers have long tried to discover some key that might show why the past had to happen the way it did, and might also afford an equally certain prediction for the future. Accordingly, they have generally proposed theories of determinism or predestination, asserting that the whole course of history is rigorously controlled by some law or power. The explanations might differ—they range from the will of God in the philosophy of St. Augustine to the necessities of economics in the philosophy of Karl Marx—but the deterministic theories are alike in holding that the individual cannot significantly alter the path of events.

A crude variety of determinism is the view that events occurred in the past simply for the purpose of creating the present situation. This is the *teleological fallacy*—the implied belief that it is the end (Greek *telos*) that brings about the chain of events, rather than the causes operating beforehand. This underlies the popular notion of "progress," and frequently creeps into the nationalistic presentation of a country's history, with the suggestion that events in the past were bound to happen the way they did in order to produce the present as it actually is. The trouble is that the actors in history are not conscious of the trend to which they may be contributing, but are usually responding to short-run considerations. For example, the "westward movement" in the history of the United States is often described as though it were a conscious mass effort at "building America" as we now know it, when in reality the "movement" is a summation we make mentally of the efforts of thousands of individuals mainly to better their personal economic circumstances.

Sweeping deterministic theories of history actually go beyond the scope of a scientific law. Gravity doesn't say I *will* fall to the ground tomorrow, but that I *will* fall *downward if* for some reason I fall at all; biology doesn't predict that I *will* die at 74, my life expectancy, but only that I am likely to, and more likely *if* I smoke too much in the meantime. In the same way, most scientific laws only state conditions or probabilities, with plenty of scope allowed for human choices. It is more fruitful to look at history this way, to seek lesser but more meaningful laws, "if . . . then" conditions, or probabilities.

We might take for an example the "law" of revolution. As a rule, revolutions begin as moderate movements and then swing to a violent extreme, usually followed by a return to moderation. The pattern has been well documented in Crane Brinton's *The Anatomy of Revolution.* Three major revolutions —the French, Russian, and Cromwell's in England—began as moderate constitutionalist protests against absolute monarchy, and all three witnessed the subsequent seizure of power by extremists who set up violent dictatorships. Here is a distinctive pattern that helps us to understand events, even though they were not absolutely determined. The "law" of revolution is not absolute, but only conditional and probable. It does not say that every country must have a revolution or that *every* revolution must display the same sequence of developments (viz., the American Revolution or the German Revolution of 1918), but the "law" does say that *if* a moderate revolution occurs, then it is *likely* to develop extremist tendencies.

A better concept than "law" in history is the idea of "model" (stressed by the famous German sociologist Max Weber). A model means some pattern of events or institutions —the "wave" of revolutionary extremism, for example—that is used as a basis for comparison or description. The model may be either an actual historical fact or an abstraction. The object is not to try to prove that all cases correspond exactly to the model, but to point out and explain the similarities and differences among the various actual cases. Why, for example, did the Russian Provisional Government fail just as did France's constitutional monarchy of 1789-1792? Why, on the other hand, was the extremist party in Russia—the Communists—never overthrown as the Jacobins were in France? Such questions bring out the uniqueness of each historical event, but also make it intelligible in terms of the total human experience.

Heroes and Accidents

If we look at history in strictly human terms, the most obvious difference from one historical situation to another is the presence of individual people, who, with their distinct personalities, behave in different and often unpredictable ways. Different individuals exercising influence in similar situations may react in opposite ways and bring about very different outcomes.

A great deal of history is taught, learned, and repeated in patriotic orations in every country to the effect that great historical events and achievements are the work of outstanding individuals. It was Thomas Carlyle who raised this attitude to the level of a philosophy with his idea of the "hero in history"—the Great Man, whose superhuman powers, wisdom, or inspiration enabled him to accomplish some fundamental change, for better or worse, in the life of his nation. In this view, any great historical step is presumed to depend on the good fortune of the Great Man's being accidentally available and achieving a position of power. Conversely, the absence of the Great Man would mean that the great event would not have occurred—no Duke of Wellington, no Waterloo; no George Washington, no United States; no Lenin, no Communism. In other words, the Great Man theory has to view history as undetermined and subject to accidental changes of course, or else the Great Man would not make any difference. (Communist historical theory is self-contradictory on this, in holding at one and the same time that the victory of Communism in Russia was inevitable but that Lenin's heroic leadership was essential to the victory.)

If the role of great leaders is decisive, it then becomes necessary to take account of the hosts of minor, accidental, unpredictable circumstances that by their presence or absence affect what the leaders do. Suppose Napoleon's will was not fogged by a cold on the eve of the Battle of Waterloo? Suppose General Grant had in fact been killed in 1863? Suppose . . . . The game could go on endlessly. The real problem is to gauge what *was* effected through an actual accident or personal decision, and what *might* have been effected through a different accident or decision.

Here we face a basic issue that historians and philosophers have never been able to settle. Is history really a chaotic stream of accidents, unpredictable both in their occurrence and their consequences? Or does it have some inner sense, some basic plan of development that governs the evolution of countries and civilizations despite all the random lesser events that garnish the historical record? Accidents do happen, but do they make a great difference in the long run? Is not much of history determined or limited by general social laws? What scope is there for an accident to have consequences or for an individual's action and decisions to matter?

If everything were chaos and accident, accidents would not matter, since new ones could constantly throw the course of events askew. For an accident or an individual to be important, it must have some governing influence on successive events—it must limit the significance of other accidents or individuals. Napoleon lost the Battle of Waterloo partly by accident, but once lost, victory was irretrievable. The entire distribution of international power had changed beyond the scope of further individual effort. France was so badly beaten that never again could she alone challenge the international balance of Europe. In the same way, Lee's defeat at Gettysburg ended the chances of the Confederacy for ultimate victory.

While an individual—Napoleon or Wellington, Lee or Grant—may exert decisive influence at certain points in history, his impact is still bound to be limited. What he can or cannot accomplish, what choices he can or cannot make successfully are more or less set by the historical circumstances of time and place. No ruler or leader, however willfull, can force himself on a million subjects and change their ways without some kind of instrument of pressure and influence, some organized system of power.

The organization of power, in all societies since the dawn of civilization, is very complex. Its most obvious element is the government, backed by the men and weapons that it has at its disposal, but including in modern Western societies the intricate web of law and the legal process. Outside of government are the economic power of business and property and the psychological power of ideas, religion, and mass communication. All these, and their particular weight at given times and places, are the product of long historical evolution. No leader, however great, can create a system of power where none exists—at best he must grasp, adapt, and utilize what he finds already at hand.

In a totalitarian dictatorship, where the leader has undivided control over the government and the government controls the economic and psychological instruments of power as well, almost everything the leader does will be decisive. Hitler and Stalin are obvious cases in point. In a democracy, with its constitutional restraints, the leader must be an exceptional man in exceptional circumstances to accomplish now what might be done sooner or later by some other servant of the electorate. In sum, the chance for leaders to have great influence depends on the nature of society, even though the

question of *which* individual gets the power may be an accident of inheritance or election. It is the rare man—a Luther or
a Lenin—who brings about fundamental changes in the very
nature of power. But even where revolutionary changes, such
as those represented by Protestantism or Communism, have
occurred, we should look for an historical explanation—perhaps weaknesses in the old organization of power that per-
mitted the great leader to break it up and rebuild it. In the
last analysis, it is the historical situation that permits the
Great Man to do his work. But the situation never guarantees
the presence of the particular individual or the direction that
he may take. So long as mankind exists, the human factor
will make history at least partially unpredictable.

Motivation

Once we recognize that individuals may play a certain role in
shaping history, whether as leaders or as part of the masses,
the quest for explanation requires us to find out why they
behave as they do. What are the motives that account for the

history-making efforts of great leaders, or that make the masses respond or refuse to respond? Which motives do all people have in common, and which are peculiar to certain individuals? How much do motives, real as they may be, actually account for what men accomplish?

It has been common to try to explain human behavior on the basis of one fundamental motive. Some say it is economic—to gain money and goods; some might say it is power —to dominate and control other people; some say devotion to a religious cause or philosophical ideal, or the group instincts of patriotism and nationalism, or psychological impulses of the libido, or whatever. Actually, none of these basic motivations can be ignored. Motivation, in real life, is a complex mixture of factors, although the mixture may differ depending on the time, the place, and the particular individual. Further, different motives may stand out among different members of a group. It is quite wrong to think, as students so often do, of "the people" as one united mass with one common desire. The problem of motivation in history is not to settle on one factor as the fundamental explanation of everyone's behavior, but to assess the particular combination of motives of each individual in each historical instance.

A good example of the mixture of motives is the ambitious politician who wants to get into power (perhaps by election, perhaps by revolution) in order to carry out an ideal or program to which he is committed. Take Lenin, for instance. The historian who believes in the guiding role of ideas would say that Lenin's real motive was the ideal Marxist program of the classless society, and that he sought power through revolution in order to carry out this program. The historian who sees all politics as the pursuit of power would say that power itself was Lenin's goal and that his ideal program was only the propagandistic excuse. This view, that ideals are manipulated to justify and serve the power motive, has been very popular among European and American social scientists in the past few decades, following the writings of the Italian sociologists Pareto and Mosca.

But it is neither necessary nor accurate to stress one motive to the detriment of others. The motives of power and ideal can be interwoven, so that the politician honestly believes that his program depends on his winning power, and that his power is justified by his program. Lenin certainly thought this way. The economic motive may be similarly involved with other impulses. Lenin was very little affected by personal economic interests, but economic grievances of the peasants and workers had much to do with his success in winning followers, and Russia's economic problems had a major effect in hardening Lenin's regime after he took power.

The economic motive is the most commonly overemphasized. It is associated with the philosophy of Marxism, though actually Marx shared this approach with many other nineteenth-century thinkers. His theory of history did not maintain that everyone was motivated mainly by economics, but rather that economic needs and resources conditioned whatever else was happening in social, political, or intellectual life. His essential point was that the different economic interests of the people with property and those without split them into hostile classes, bound to struggle until eventually the institution of private property would be abolished.

It is quite possible to stress economic factors in history without being a Marxist and without believing in the class struggle. In fact, the nineteenth-century tradition of laissez-faire, individualist economics, which is still strong in the United States, puts heavy emphasis on the economic motive of profit-seeking. Historians have frequently sought economic motives in historical situations where the apparent impulse was very different—religious fervor in the Reformation, for example, or nationalistic hatreds in World War I. Still, a great deal has to be explained by very impractical motives and irrational impulses, though the philosophy of eighteenth-century rationalism in which American thinking is largely grounded takes little account of such factors. Because American history has been relatively free from the passions of hate and fear, the bonds of tradition and authority, the horrors of insane despots and wanton devastation, there is all the more need for the American student to try to recognize these negative and irrational facets of the human experience through the study of other areas of the world.

Perhaps the most subtle problem in assessing historical motivation is to weigh its results. The fact that an individual tries to do something for a certain reason is no guarantee that he will achieve the result he desires. A political leader only adds his decision or actions to the host of factors, institutional forces, and mass emotions already present in a given situation. He must hope that he understands the situation well enough to make the kind of decision that will help to realize his motivation. Otherwise his efforts may even backfire. Neville Chamberlain was most certainly motivated by the desire for peace in 1938, but his fearful, vacillating decisions only assured the onset of war under conditions that were nearly fatal for his side.

Because the stream of history is so complex and unpredictable, it is always risky to seek a direct relationship between motive and result. Looking back from the result, it is equally unsure to assume that the makers of history intended what they accomplished. The American colonists and pioneers may indeed have contributed to building America, but this is not to say that they felt they were struggling for a future national plan more than for their personal salvation or prosperity. The results of the historical process are at any point the product of a vast interplay of factors and circumstances in which the conscious motives and actions of individuals are only a small part.

The Interaction of Historical Factors

In speaking of motivation in history, we have used terms that correspond closely to the different levels of historical activity. The coincidence is natural, for we are analyzing the various ways in which people act and the areas of their interests—the realms of politics, economic activity, social life, and ideological or religious beliefs. Naturally these levels of historical experience are interconnected. Governmental decisions may influence the economy; economic changes may create a crisis for the government; intellectual developments—in science, for instance—may lead to revolutionary changes in economics

and social life. Most of the laws of historical causation are essentially theories about how these levels of history interact and influence each other.

The simplest kind of historical law is a one-factor explanation. It asserts that one aspect of history is decisive, that it determines everything important going on in all the other aspects. Marx based his theory on the dominant influence of the "mode of production," i.e., economic circumstances. Economics, in his view, determined the organization of society into classes; and, in turn, the particular ruling class decided the character of the government and imposed its system of belief, religion, or philosophy on the rest of society. Equally convincing arguments can be made, however, for the primacy of other factors. Hegel believed that the realm of ideas was decisive, and that a guiding "world spirit" determined the rise and fall of nations. (Marx had borrowed Hegel's "dialectical" or developmental approach, but with a shift of emphasis from the ideal to the material. He remarked that he had found Hegel "standing on his head and turned him right side up again.") The belief that great leaders are the decisive makers of history is a political theory of history, which assumes that decisive change comes from government. Most of the eighteenth-century philosophers were inclined to some form of political emphasis, and viewed the inspired leader or constitution or legislation as decisive. Montesquieu went a step further, with an interesting theory of geographical determinism; he held that the success of government depended on choosing the form corresponding to the size and climate of the country.

The trouble with these one-factor approaches is that they all have a measure of truth; none, therefore, can be absolutely true by itself. The different factors in history constantly affect each other through interaction and mutual influence, making history all the more complicated and unpredictable.

Granting this ongoing interaction, it is still possible to look for a greater contribution by one factor in a particular situation. Where was a given novelty initiated before its consequences grew through the interaction among many factors? Take the atomic bomb. It could not have been developed without the intellectual (scientific) and political (governmental) factors. But initially and independently came the scientific discoveries in nuclear physics, without which the vast political and military consequences of nuclear weapons could never have occurred. In this instance we are compelled to say that science was the initial causative factor in an historic change.

Another way to assign primary importance is to ask which factor has more weight as the interaction progresses, which has more influence in the long run. Government can influence the economy by its regulations and tax policies, but in the long run the development of the economy and the economic interests of the citizenry probably have an even greater influence on what government tries to do. Interaction may thus be unbalanced, as the novelties in one aspect of history ultimately shape the development of the other aspects.

Finally, different factors may have primary influence, depending on the time and place. Religious commitments and disputes were decisive in the era of the Reformation, but have usually been subordinate since then. Economic interests and changes have been decisive in the modern history of Western Europe and North America, but not as much in Russia. Russian

Russia

history since the Middle Ages has been distinguished by the dominant influence of politics, as political events and governmental decisions largely shaped (and often stunted) the development of the other aspects of life. This remains true in Soviet Russia today, despite the official Marxist philosophy with its emphasis on the role of economics. Nor is philosophy the guiding factor in Soviet society, but rather an instrument to justify the policies developed in the political power structure.

Predicting or Shaping the Future?

Just as the present is the product of the historical factors, individual decisions, and accidents of the past, so the future is the product of the present. To the student of history who has learned how to understand the way this process has worked, it is naturally tempting to apply the same methods to forecast the future.

From the historian's standpoint, the prediction of future events is not crystal ball gazing. It must be a serious effort to foresee what is likely to continue or develop out of the circumstances of the present, and to anticipate future problems and opportunities. Actually, all men are constantly doing this, whether or not they are consciously aware of it. They simply try to plan actions that will alter the course of events for the better, or at least reduce the chances of some unfortunate occurrence.

Planning and foresight depend on learning by experience. For statesmen, this means applying the "lessons of history," with due regard for what these lessons do and do not teach. The trouble with lessons of history is that they rely on the parallel between a new situation and earlier ones, thus assuming that history is fundamentally static. In fact, of course, the world changes, and an apparently similar situation may require very different responses. For example, in the 1930s the United States tried to apply the lessons of World War I by passing the neutrality acts to avoid involvement in a European war. The results, under the new circumstances of the

Nazi challenge, were the failure to help prevent World War II and the prolongation of the struggle at bitter cost to the world. Someone has said that "the only lesson history teaches is that history never teaches any lessons."

When we speak of statesmanship and the lessons of history, we have in mind the effort to make wise decisions about the future on the basis of knowledge about the past and present. This implies that present decisions can have an effect on determining the future, along with the forces bequeathed by what is now the past. The future depends on what people decide, what they attempt, what they accidentally accomplish or fail to accomplish. Here is the real limitation on any prediction—the future is still, to one degree or another, indeterminate. It is not wholly "in the cards," subject to the scrutiny of some clairvoyant. It has not yet been decided.

What does decide the future is a combination of factors—the historical forces and circumstances of the past and present, which we can try to weigh and assess, and the human decisions and responses that have not yet been made. Thus the future is partly knowable and partly unknowable, in proportions that historians will disagree over. Those who emphasize the economic and social factors, involving the interests and responses of masses of people, will feel that the future is largely determined for some time ahead by the present momentum of historical tendencies that have been going on in the past. Those who emphasize the role of leaders, the political power structure, or intellectual innovations will regard the future as much more unpredictable, because it is subject to individual actions and inspirations that cannot be foreseen.

In any case, the shape of the future is partly governed by human actions and intentions, and to this extent the question is not what we predict, but what we want. Or rather, given the forces of historical development that are now in process, what decisions can we make or recommend that will yield the best practicable course for the future? In other words, when the study of history is turned toward the future, it becomes the subject of policy—the choice and pursuit of the goals at which a society will aim.

When a leader occupies a position where he can make such choices and secure the implementation of them, we can say that he is able to "make history." His role and its success will be affected and limited by many conditions, of course. The entire political and social situation emanating from the past restricts his alternatives. He must have some organized instrument of power—usually the government—to swing the responses of his society and alter what might otherwise have been the flow of events. His power might be autocratic, with his word as law, or democratic, subject to the approval of the voters, or purely inspirational, such as that of a religious or literary leader who has no formal organization of power at his command. The greatest political leaders combine inspirational with political authority. Hitler and Churchill are perfect examples—one of inspirational-autocratic, the other of inspirational-democratic influence. In any case, history-making leadership depends on the particular chances that bring together a man who wants to lead and decide, and the machinery that can translate his will into an historic change for the whole of society.

There is one final kind of limitation on the history-making effect of leadership and policy. This is a point we noted earlier in assessing the historic role of individuals—that policy may not produce the intended results. There is a long chain between intention, policy decision, leadership action, social response, and historic result. In the effort to shape history by policy decision, so many slips are possible that an unintended result is highly probable. Hitler promised a "Thousand Year Reich"; because of his miscalculations, his regime lasted only twelve years and three months. Whatever leaders or governments do, their action is just one more factor tossed into the kaleidoscope of historical forces, and even with the best of insight and foresight the leader can never be sure that his plans will work out as he hopes. Marx's collaborator, Friedrich Engels, once wrote: "People who boasted that they had *made* a revolution have always seen the next day that they had no idea what they were doing, that the revolution *made* did not in the least resemble the one they would have liked to make." Some of the most elaborate political programs—

Russia

notably, the revolutionary ideology of communism—have mis-fired very badly in terms of their original objectives, because the leaders did not fully understand the circumstances in which they were acting and the effect that their actions would have. The best statesman is the man with a good historical sense of the unpredictable and the ironic, who does the best he can in the knowledge that it may not work and who above all keeps his mind flexible, so that his objectives will not be undermined by rigidly held policies that are not succeeding. John F. Kennedy came close to the mark.

CONCLUSION:
HISTORY
AND VALUES

IN THIS BRIEF BOOK I have tried to show how the study of history can contribute to the formation of the educated person, either as a major subject of study or as a supplement to other fields of the liberal arts. History is an indispensable part of the liberal education that aspires to train the general powers of the mind and open it to an awareness of the greatest things that men have done, thought, or discovered. From history comes a breadth of experience that is matched in no other way, to achieve awareness of different kinds of life in other times and places. It furnishes perspective on the moving forces of the present and the only basis for intelligent decisions about future action. It is a major source of the values, commitments, and excitement that make life worth living, that make man human.

With respect to utility, history perhaps has its major value in training the student how to think, in ways that carry over into almost every other subject or activity. We might summarize here the thought processes that have been explained in each chapter of this book.

Chapter 1 outlines some of the attitudes of mind that come with historical study. Among these are the sense of change and process, the spirit of objectivity and curiosity, recognition of the relativity of values, and the perspective of mature citizenship.

In Chapter 2 the fields of history are explained—chronological, geographical, and topical—as classifications for ordering all human experience. Understanding such a structure makes it possible to look at any complex subject with some clarity and organization, and also flexibility.

Chapter 3 assesses the nature of history in relation to the other disciplines of knowledge. History as a social science has to take account of the values and uncertainty in human affairs that science cannot reach. For this reason and because it encompasses all the separate activities treated by the other social sciences and humanities, history is the most comprehensive approach to human affairs.

In Chapter 4, I have taken a more practical turn, to guide the student in his actual acquisition of historical knowledge and understanding. I have tried to expound an approach to the understanding of details, generalizations, and relationships that might carry over to any work of acquiring knowledge.

The next two chapters continue the practical, with emphasis on the most demanding and also most rewarding sides of historical work—writing and research. These skills are of course not confined to history, though history requires real competence in them and is second to none as a training experience in them. Historical writing teaches the logic of thought; historical research teaches the nature of humanistic knowledge and judgment. Together research and writing train a person to know and evaluate his world and to communicate his knowledge and values to his fellows.

On the basis of all the foregoing analysis, Chapter 7 introduces the reader to the interpretation of history—the how and why of the course of events. Here the subject becomes particularly complex, because it requires recognition of possibilities and probabilities as well as certainties, and a sense of context and proportion regarding all the personal and abstract factors in the development of society. The work of interpreting and assessing historical causes and motives is consequently the key experience for a student in cultivating the values of the historical approach.

The record of history is far more than a chronicle of events. It not only records what people have done, but also what they have tried to do, the motives and goals that impelled them to strive for something better. History is a repository of human values and aspirations, the accumulation of efforts, experience, hopes, and achievements that have gradually civilized humanity. We must know history to be aware of our evolving human nature, both the worst and the best in it.

There is an inevitable tension in the study of history between the detachment required by the subject, and the natural attraction and repulsion exercised by the powerful values that are encountered in it. History is a manifold source of inspiration through every kind of exciting episode and dyna-

mic leader, and a major value of history would be lost if the
student refused altogether to be involved with the passions
and struggles of the past. Who can fail to be excited and
prodded, for instance, by Jacob Burckhardt's vivid evocation
of the super-alive "Renaissance man" in his classic, The
Civilization of the Renaissance in Italy? Who is there who
will not simmer with indignation at the story of Roman slavery
or the seventeenth-century "witchcraft" executions? Historians
as a group have not let their critical training undermine their
capacity to become involved with values and causes that on
balance they judge worthy of their personal commitment.

But there is one important qualification that history
teaches: caution against overly simple commitment to values,
past or present. The historical approach requires us to recognize that human values are not based on a single standard,
but are inherently diverse, both from time to time and from
place to place. History develops a sense of relativity about
values—that good and evil, progress and retrogression, must
be judged in relation to the circumstances of time and place.
Was medieval serfdom all bad? It was better than Roman
slavery, and it provided the economic foundation for military
defense and a cultural revival. Is Communism all bad? Or
should it be judged as a path to a modern economy in countries that would probably not be democratic in any case?
Many more questions could be raised to show that pure values
rarely occur in practice, but are usually found mixed in various shades of gray.

There is another complication in most historical situations
—the discrepancy between ideals and actions, between theory
and practice. Historical realism requires us to recognize that
people do not always do what they think or say they ought
to do, and when they do pursue their values, they do not
always achieve their goal. History is the record of imperfection, but it is also the record of potential.

The story of human progress is awe-inspiring when one
reflects that it was not inevitable or foreordained. Why, at a
particular point in mankind's million-year biological existence,
did civilization suddenly appear? Why, in the modern West,
did the intellectual powers, technical accomplishments, and

moral consciousness of man expand so phenomenally? There was no cosmic reason for any of this. It was the result of human effort—often short-sighted, often frustrated, certainly not mindful of our present, let alone of our future, but all the same, effort that created phenomena of civilization and culture that so far as we know are unmatched in the universe. The obvious dangers and imperfections of the present should not blind us to this perspective. The human adventure has been a fantastic one, and there is no limit to what it may achieve in epochs yet to come, should it survive the perils of man's own technical ingenuity.

Suggestions for Further Reading

Useful Guides to Study and Research

Barzun, Jacques, and Henry Graff, *The Modern Researcher.* New York: Harcourt Brace Jovanovich, 1957.

Bruner, Jerome, *The Process of Education.* Cambridge, Mass.: Harvard University Press, 1961.

Gray, Wood, *Historian's Handbook: A Key to the Writing and Study of History.* Boston: Houghton Mifflin, 1964.

Handlin, Oscar, et al., *Harvard Guide to American History.* Cambridge, Mass.: Harvard University Press, 1954.

Howe, George Frederick, et. al., eds., *The American Historical Association's Guide to Historical Literature.* New York: Macmillan, 1961.

Langer, William L., ed., *An Encyclopedia of World History.* Boston: Houghton Mifflin, 1968.

Nevins, Allan, *The Gateway to History.* New York: Doubleday, 1962.

Whitehead, Alfred North, *The Aims of Education.* New York: Macmillan, 1929.

Books on the Nature of History

Becker, Carl, *Everyman His Own Historian.* New York: Appleton-Century-Crofts, 1935.

Berkhofer, Robert F. Jr., *A Behavioral Approach to Historical Analysis.* New York: Free Press, 1969.

Bloch, Marc, *The Historian's Craft.* New York: Knopf, 1953.

Bober, Mandell, *Karl Marx's Interpretation of History.* Cambridge, Mass.: Harvard University Press, 1927.

Butterfield, Herbert, *The Whig Interpretation of History.* London: G. Bell, 1951.

Cahnman, Werner, and Alvin Boskoff, eds., *Sociology and History.* New York: Free Press, 1964.

Carlyle, Thomas, *On Heroes, Hero-Worship and the Heroic in History*. New York: Oxford University Press, 1928.

Carr, Edward Hallett, *What is History?* New York: Knopf, 1962.

Collingwood, R. G., *The Idea of History*. New York: Oxford University Press, 1946.

Dray, William, *The Philosophy of History*. Englewood Cliffs, N.J.: Prentice-Hall, 1965.

Gottschalk, Louis, *Understanding History: A Primer of Historical Method*. New York: Knopf, 1950.

Gustavson, Carl G., *A Preface to History*. New York: McGraw-Hill, 1955.

Holt, W. S., *The Historical Profession in the United States*. Washington, Service Center for Teachers of History (American Historical Assn.), publication no. 52, 1963.

Hook, Sidney, *The Hero in History*. New York: Humanities Press, 1950.

Hughes, H. Stuart, *Consciousness and Society: The Reorientation of European Social Thought, 1890-1930*. New York: Knopf, 1958.

Koht, Halvdan, *Driving Forces in History*. Cambridge, Mass.: Harvard University Press, 1964.

Landes, David S., and Charles Tilly, eds., *History as Social Science*. Englewood Cliffs, N.J.: Prentice-Hall, 1971.

Shafer, Boyd C., et. al., *Historical Study in the West*. New York: Appleton-Century-Crofts, 1968.

Spengler, Oswald, *The Decline of the West* (2 vols.). New York: Knopf, 1945.

Stern, Fritz, ed., *The Varieties of History from Voltaire to the Present*. New York: World Publishing Co., 1956.

Toynbee, Arnold, *A Study of History* (Abridged ed., 2 vols.). New York: Oxford University Press, 1946, 1957.

Works on Illustrative Historical Subjects

Bainton, Roland, *Here I Stand: A Life of Martin Luther*. Nashville, Tenn.: Abingdon, 1950.

Baldwin, Marshall W., *The Medieval Church*. Ithaca, N.Y.: Cornell University Press, 1950.

Boak, Arthur E. R., *A History of Rome to 565 A.D.* New York: Macmillan, 1955.

Brinton, Crane, *The Anatomy of Revolution.* Englewood Cliffs, N.J.: Prentice-Hall, 1952.

Brinton, Crane, John B. Christopher, and Robert L. Wolff, *A History of Civilization* (2 vols.). Englewood Cliffs, N.J.: Prentice-Hall, 1960.

Bruun, Geoffrey, *The Enlightened Despots.* New York: Holt, Rinehart and Winston, 1929.

Bullock, Alan, *Hitler: A Study in Tyranny.* New York: Harper and Row, 1952.

Burckhardt, Jacob, *The Civilization of the Renaissance in Italy.* New York: Modern Library, 1954.

Bury, John B., *History of Greece to the Death of Alexander.* London: Macmillan, 1951.

Butterfield, Herbert, *The Origins of Modern Science, 1500-1800.* New York: The Macmillan Company, 1951.

Careless, James M. S., *Canada: A Story of Challenge.* New York: St. Martin's, 1963.

Catton, Bruce, *The Centennial History of the Civil War* (3 vols.). New York: Doubleday, 1961-1963.

Clough, Shepard, *Economic History of Europe.* Lexington, Mass.: Raytheon/Heath, 1947.

Cowles, Virginia, *Winston Churchill: The Era and the Man.* New York: Harper and Row, 1953.

Curtiss, John S., *An Appraisal of the Protocols of Zion.* New York: Columbia University Press, 1942.

Daniels, Robert, ed., *Marxism and Communism: Essential Readings.* New York: Random House, 1965.

————, *The Nature of Communism.* New York: Random House, 1962.

————, *Red October: The Bolshevik Revolution of 1917.* New York: Scribner's, 1967.

Deutscher, Isaac, *Stalin: A Political Biography.* New York: Oxford University Press, 1949.

Ferguson, Wallace K., *The Renaissance in Historical Thought.* Boston: Houghton Mifflin, 1948.

Fischer, Louis, *The Life of Lenin.* New York: Harper and Row, 1964.

Fisher, Herbert A. L., *Napoleon.* London: Oxford University Press, 1912.

Fisher, Sidney N., *The Middle East: A History.* Ann Arbor: University of Michigan Press, 1959.

Florinsky, Michael T., *Russia: A History and an Interpretation* (2 vols.), New York: Macmillan, 1953.

Franklin, John Hope, *From Slavery to Freedom: A History of Negro Americans,* 3rd ed. New York: Knopf, 1969.

Grebler, Leo, Joan W. Moore, and Ralph C. Guzman, *The Mexican-American People.* New York: Free Press, 1970.

Halecki, Oscar, *A History of Poland.* New York: Roy, 1956.

Hall, Walter, Robert Albion, and Jennie Pope, *A History of England and the Empire-Commonwealth.* Boston: Ginn, 1961.

Havens, George R., *The Age of Ideas: From Reaction to Revolution in Eighteenth-Century France.* New York: Holt, Rinehart and Winston, 1955.

Herring, Hubert, *A History of Latin America.* New York: Knopf, 1960.

Hofstadter, Richard, William Miller, and Daniel Aaron, *The Structure of American History.* Englewood Cliffs, N.J.: Prentice-Hall, 1961.

Hughes, H. Stuart, *Contemporary Europe: A History.* Englewood Cliffs, N.J.: Prentice-Hall, 1961.

Kantor, MacKinlay, *If the South Had Won the Civil War.* New York: Bantam, 1961.

Latourette, Kenneth Scott, *China.* Englewood Cliffs, N.J.: Prentice-Hall, 1965.

Lefebvre, Georges, *The Coming of the French Revolution.* New York: Random House, 1957.

———, *The French Revolution from Its Origins to 1793.* New York: Columbia University Press, 1962.

Lucas, Henry S., *The Renaissance and the Reformation.* New York: Harper and Row, 1960.

Mathiez, Albert, *The French Revolution.* New York: Russell Sage Foundation, 1962.

Mattingly, Garrett, *The Armada.* Boston: Houghton Mifflin, 1959.

Montesquieu, Charles de Secondat, Baron, *The Spirit of Laws.* Chicago: Encyclopaedia Britannica, 1955.

Oliver, Roland, and J. D. Tage, *A Short History of Africa.* Baltimore: Penguin, 1962.

Randall, John H., Jr., *The Making of the Modern Mind.* Boston: Houghton Mifflin, 1940.

Reischauer, Edwin O., *Japan, Past and Present.* New York: Knopf, 1953.

Rodes, John E., *Germany: A History.* New York: Holt, Rinehart and Winston, 1964.

Schachner, Nathan, *The Founding Fathers.* New York: Putnam's, 1954.

Starkey, Marion, *The Devil in Massachusetts.* New York: Knopf, 1949.

Stavrianos, Leften, S., *The Balkans Since 1453.* New York: Holt, Rinehart and Winston, 1963.

Strayer, Joseph, and Dana C. Munro, *The Middle Ages: 395-1500.* New York: Appleton-Century-Crofts, 1959.

Taine, Hippolyte, *The French Revolution* (3 vols.). New York: Holt, Rinehart and Winston, 1878-1885.

Taylor, Alan J. P., *The Origins of World War Two.* New York: Atheneum, 1962.

Thomas, Benjamin P., *Abraham Lincoln: A Biography.* New York: Knopf, 1952.

Thompson, James M., *Robespierre and the French Revolution.* New York: Macmillan, 1953.

Wallbank, T. Walter, *A Short History of India and Pakistan.* New York: New American Library, 1958.

Wright, Gordon, *France in Modern Times.* Skokie, Ill.: Rand McNally, 1960.